Flagging:
An Audience Unto One

Giving God All Your Worship

Marcia Loofboro

Flagging: An Audience Unto One

**Published by
Dove Christian Publishers
P.O. Box 611
Bladensburg, MD 20710-0611
www.dovechristianpublishers.com**

Copyright © 2020 by Marcia Loofboro

Cover Design by Sandy Lucas

All rights reserved. No part of this publication may be used or reproduced without permission of the publisher, except for brief quotes for scholarly use, reviews or articles.

Scripture quotations marked NLT, New Living Translation, are taken from the *Holy Bible,* New Living Translation, copyright 1996. Used by permission of Tyndale House Publishers, Inc., Wheaton, Illinois 60189. All rights reserved.

Scripture quotations marked TPT are from The Passion Translation®. Copyright © 2017, 2018 by Passion & Fire Ministries, Inc. Used by permission. All rights reserved. ThePassionTranslation.com.

Author's Note: I have capitalized certain pronouns in Scripture that refer to the Father, Son, and the Holy Spirit and may differ from the publisher's style. Also, the name satan and related names are not capitalized. I chose not to acknowledge him even to the point of violating grammatical rules. All emphasis within scripture quotations is the author's own.

Andrea York of Catch the Fire Worship Flags.com has given me permission to use her materials from her classroom and videos on YouTube in this book.

Rosie Boyden Robinson has given me permission to publish her interview with Clarstar Films from 9-2-19, found on Facebook.

ISBN: 9781734303216

Printed in the United States of America

Flags

*Flags - yellow, orange & gold
Red, blue & purple too.
All to give You glory Lord
To show our love for You.
Flowing, moving in love divine
Fighting in the heavenlies with glory divine.
Warfare for His cause
To bring to earth His purpose and not loss.
A joy to flag for you today -
glory and praise be on their way.*

Table of Contents

Introduction v

Chapter 1 3
    What is Flagging about? Worship!

Chapter 2 11
    Is Flagging Scriptural?

Chapter 3 17
    Our Authority

Chapter 4 32
    The Blessing

Chapter 5 39
    The Baptism of the Holy Spirit

Chapter 6 49
    Spirit, Soul & Body

Chapter 7 54
    Communion

Chapter 8 64
    Types of Flags, Rods, Moves

Chapter 9 69
    Colors, Naming, Scriptural References

Chapter 10 74
    How to Make a Basic Flag

Chapter 11 79
    References for Making or Purchasing Flags

Endnotes 84

Introduction

I felt from the Lord to write a book about flagging after He brought it back into my life in February of 2019 when I got to flag for a few minutes at a women's conference. I had flagged previously but not had the opportunity for a number of years. When I got my hands on a set of flags, all of that changed. I remembered what it was like to flag, and forward I went again. I bought my first few sets of flags, then I began making them for myself and for sharing. I've shared them with a number of people, giving them the opportunity to worship Our Lord through flagging as well.

But this book is more than just about flagging. There are spiritual concepts that truly need to be understood in the Body of Christ today. So by the Lord's prompting, I have added some basic teaching on these other important concepts, which are *the Believer's Authority, the Blessing, Spirit, Soul and Body, the Baptism of the Holy Spirit* and *Communion*.

Also included in this book is some information on how to make your own flags, where to find supplies, and many reference sources to help you along the way. You may connect more with the flags you prophetically make for yourself, using colors and scriptures that the Lord is putting in your heart. You will find you will have different flags for the different seasons in your life, connecting to what you are doing and what is going on in your life and ministry at those times.

I am thankful for all the help I received online learning the correct concepts and uses of flags and how to make them. I am especially thankful for all the help I found on Andrea York's website "Catch the Fire" and in her classroom that really helped me get started. I will list these sources in the reference section of Part 2, *The Mechanics of Flag Making*. I don't remember where I got every detail, but thank you all for your help.

I hope this book is a blessing to you in finding your deeper walk in the Lord through a better understanding of the benefits of our heritage and through flagging. I will add references to books I've read and CDs I've listened to that have helped me understand and write about these spiritual principles included in this book.

Here is one of the poems the Lord gave me soon after I started making my own flags:

Flagging

Flagging - a joy to bring
Worship to my King
Yellow, blue, green and white
Transformed in His sight
Joy for me, Love for Him
Flagging helps me move in Him
Standing up or sitting in my chair
Moving joyfully without a care
Up and down, around we go
Showing our love to Him from us below
Glory, Glory to Him may be
Lasting love to share with Thee
You are mine and I am His
The joy of love to forever give
So raise your banners high to Thee
Worship Him upon your knees
His mercy will bless you forevermore
Glory shine from shore to shore

Part 1: Worship
(Kissing the Hand)

*Daily I will worship you passionately and with all my heart.
My arms will wave to you like banners of praise.
I overflow with praise when I come before you,
for the anointing of your Presence satisfies me like nothing else.
You are such a rich banquet of pleasure to my soul
(Psalm 63:4-5 TPT)*

Chapter 1

What is Flagging about? Worship!

Flagging is a form of worship, giving ourselves over to honoring, experiencing and loving on Him. But what is worship? It is the only right response to the Lord. When you know the Lord, you worship the Lord. The definition of worship from the Merriam-Webster online dictionary is, as a noun, *a reverence offered a divine being or supernatural power; an act of expressing such reverence.* As a verb, it is *to honor or show reverence for a divine being or supernatural power.* So, as we worship, we give our reverence and our honor to someone who is greater than us. Worship is agreeing with who He is, seeing the Lord rightly. In Andrea York's teaching on worship[1], she defines true worship as "accurately seeing God as He is and responding to Him. Worship is not an event but an intimate experience of God." We worship who He is and praise Him for what He has done. Worship is getting our eyes off of ourselves, off our mission to where we began beholding the beauty of the man Jesus. It takes precedence over everything else.[2] Worship is what marked David's life as we see in Ps 27:4:

> "The one thing I ask of the Lord—the thing I seek most—is to live in the house of the Lord all the days of my life, delighting in the Lord's perfections and meditating in his Temple."

Worship frees us. For we exist in Him and He in us; we are sustained by His breath for we cannot live one second without Him. The Father breathed His life into the first man Adam, and He continually sustains us now by His light and His breath. If He removed His breath and His light from this universe, we would cease to exist. The first act of creation was putting Himself back into the earth, bringing order out of formlessness and chaos (Genesis 1:2). So when we worship and accurately see Him as He is, we are the freest, because we are acting more like Him. We want to be in intimate, close fellowship with Him and He with us. Intimacy is mutually beneficial because it benefits both parties. He intends for us to have supernatural experiences and live supernaturally in our lives through Him.[3]

In Revelation 4:8, we find the four living creatures singing *"Holy, holy, holy is the Lord God, the Almighty—the one who always was, who is, and who is still to come."* The four living creatures are full of eyes, constantly looking on God; He is always in their view. We must keep God always in our view. He is to be our focus. He invites us to continually worship Him. He is our victory over any type of bondage in our lives. God told Moses He would always be with Him after the Lord told him to take His people out of Egypt. This was a promise of a relationship and a promise of victory.

Worship transforms us. When you are transformed through worship, you influence and transform the culture around you by who you are. For as born-again believers, we are ambassadors for the Kingdom, being His hands and His feet in this world. For God precedes every move He asks you to do. If He calls you somewhere, He will precede you and provide all that you will need and more. In Ps 68:12, we see that a war had been going on, and after the victory, the enemy flees and the women are left to gather the spoils. God called Moses to lead His people out of Egypt, and there was not one feeble among them, spoiling the Egyptians, giving them more than enough for their journey.

Chapter 1: What is Flagging about? Worship!

We drive out evil with our worship. It is called the law of displacement. When something with more power and substance comes in, it will drive out the lesser. God is always greater than our adversary, the devil.

When Moses went up the mountain and worshipped and fellowshipped with the Lord, he was transformed and his face shone. Exodus 34:29-30 NLT:

> *"When Moses came down Mount Sinai carrying the two stone tablets inscribed with the terms of the covenant, he wasn't aware that his face had become radiant because he had spoken to the Lord. So when Aaron and the people of Israel saw the radiance of Moses' face, they were afraid to come near him."*

Not everyone was happy with Moses after he came off the mountain. Not everyone will be happy with you either. Not everyone was happy about Jesus. But we are all called to worship Him and give Him glory. So do it anyway!

In worshipping Him, we exalt and honor the Lord, lavishing our love on Him. When we flag, we flag with our whole bodies.

> *(Rom 6:13 NLT: "Use your whole body as an instrument to do what is right for the glory of God." Ps 63:4-5: "Daily I will worship you passionately with all my heart. My arms will wave to you like banners of praise. I will overflow with praise when I come before you, for the anointing of your presence satisfies me like nothing else." Habk 3-4 NLT: "I see God, the Holy One, moving across the deserts from Edom and Mount Paran. His brilliant splendor fills the heaven, and the earth is filled with His praises! What a wonderful God is He. Rays of brilliant light flash from His hands. He rejoices in His awesome power").*

Flagging without worship means nothing; it is just a performance. Comparing it to what the scripture says about prophecy, if not done in love, it is like a clanging cymbal, noise. We flag to show Him our love. Flagging is another language of worship, bringing our attention to Him. It is not about performance or showy moves; it is all about Him. Andrea York made this comment about flagging: "Worship flags are a conversation you have with God, except instead of using words you are speaking with colors." For color has a voice. We praise God for all He has done and we worship Him because of who He is (Andrea York, "Going Deeper in God" study).[4]

Things happen when we worship the Lord while flagging, but our main goal is to worship Him. When we come into His presence, it changes atmospheres, warfare happens, clogged airways and airwaves are opened up. But those are all side benefits of worship. As with music and prayer, these things can happen but the purpose of all worship is to focus on Him and His Presence. For the Presence is Jesus and our response to the Presence is our response to Him. If His Presence is a side issue, then so is Jesus. The Presence has to be the center of everything we do. As with prayer, we focus on Him, having a relational communication, saying what He is saying and moving where He is moving. It is in the Presence of Jesus that lives are transformed. When we host His Presence lives are transformed and then cities are transformed.

When we worship the Lord in flagging, we are co-laboring, co-creating with the Holy Spirit. We are entering into His Presence and allowing the Holy Spirit to work through us here on this earth. For here, we are the hands and the feet of the Lord. He, the Lord, through the Holy Spirit, lets us know what He wants to do, and by our cooperating with Him, it happens. We pray to the Father, He speaks to the Son, Jesus commands the angels and gets the work done. Our assignments are to love and be in agreement and obedience in all that we do.

Flags are tools, extensions of us, giving worship unto the Lord. They become part of us as we worship. I have actually witnessed this. The flags seemed to become part of a lady's arms as she worshipped with the flags. They became one with her. Flags can enhance our worship if used properly. And that enhanced worship can have a peaceful and healing effect on others watching.

It is not our job, with flags, to change the atmosphere in a place, for we actually do that by our very presence, in His presence. When people, who are filled with the glory of God, step onto the scene, darkness is pushed back and simultaneously confronts everything that is disconnected from God (Law of Displacement).

The glory reminds people and creation of their beginnings, of living in the glory, lost by the sin of Adam. That state of glory living has now been bought for us by the Blood of Jesus. As born again believers we have the Holy Spirit, that glory, living now on the inside of us, functioning with us, bringing honor to God:

> *(Eph 1:13-14 NLT: "And now you Gentiles have also heard the truth, the Good News that God saves you. And when you believed in Christ, He identified you as His own, by giving you the Holy Spirit, which He promised long ago. The Spirit is God's guarantee that He will give us that inheritance He promised and that He purchased us to be His own people. He did that so we would praise and glorify Him").*

Our focus is on worshipping the Lord and that worship is what changes the atmosphere. I have experienced this in places where what seemed "hard" became "open", receptive. I have experienced demonic entities leave an area by just taking my triple white flag out of its bag (White has to do with purity, holiness, righteousness, the bride of Christ).

It is important to be discerning of what is taking place in the areas where you go. We always need to keep our spiritual eyes and ears open, being receptive to the Holy

Spirit and what is happening around us. You also need to be aware of what "spirit" you are in when you go into an area. If you come into a place full of love, that love will affect the atmosphere; if you come in frustrated and angry, that will also affect the atmosphere in a detrimental way. Loves "breeds" love; anger breeds anger, discontent and strife.

Have you ever been in a room that was "light" and happy, and someone walks in and the whole sense of the room changes? This could happen with a dignitary walking in, bringing a sense of honor and the room quiets down, or someone who is angry walks in and the whole atmosphere of the room changes from happy to "ugly." My husband and I have seen this when we have done music in nursing homes. The residents could be restless when we come in, but as we do the music, they settle down and become calm and peaceful, making it much easier for the nurses to care for them. We have actually had nurses comment on how the music calmed the residents. We can change the atmosphere with our love, for love is warfare. Love drives out the enemy.

Some people like to flag with fast driving movement; my husband, for example, has pretty much one smooth flowing move. But all moves, fast or gentle, can drive out opposing forces, cleansing and clearing areas around us. It is the love behind the movement that has the effect.

You can flag to music or without it. Lots of people flag to music, allowing the music to direct their movements by the power of the Holy Spirit. I like to pray in tongues and flag, also following what I am sensing by the Spirit. My husband sings in tongues and flags. Just remember to do it all as worship unto the Lord, hosting His Presence in the room or area.

You don't have to be in a church to flag. People flag in parks, in their yards, by the river, by the ocean; you can actually flag anywhere it is lawful to be. You don't have to flag with others; you can just worship the Lord by yourself.

We flag at our house alone, we flag while watching services on our Roku or computer. As long as you have room to do it, go for it. If you just have a smaller space, you can use a smaller flag. There are many types of flags or tools with which to worship. Just worship! For it is about hosting the Presence.

Flagging is all about relationship with the Lord, for it is a privilege to carry His Presence. It is not a labor or work; it's about a relationship. The ministry of flagging should flow out of our relationship with the One who is living on the inside of us and rests upon us for the sake of ourselves and others.

When we praise with our flags, we release the Presence, for He inhabits our praises. When the Presence is released, we have given Him His rightful place. His world then collides with the world of darkness and His kingdom/world always wins. By our worship, through flagging, we cleanse our environment and ourselves by driving out the darkness with the Presence of our Almighty Lord.

Here is a testimony from Rosie Robinson from a mini interview on 9-2-19 for Clarstar Films, that she has given me permission to publish.[5]

She was asked, "What is your name and what does flag worship mean to you?"

> *"My name is Rosie Robinson and flag worship to me means a lot of things. There is not categorically like one identifiable thing that I could say that means to me. One thing, in a nutshell, flag worship means everything to me. Everything!*
>
> *"Flag worship to me is the capacity to express a language of gratitude to the Lord, of prayer, of testimony, of honor. It means the capacity, the ability to give God glory beyond my ability to speak words to Him."*

(She continues on telling about her life - but summarizing it up, flag worship is what God used in her life to save her from herself. She was able to express her sorrow and worship her way out to life. In a moment when she almost took her own life, God gave it back to her through flagging.)

Rosie continues "Each flag is a language, each flag is a statement to the Lord. Every color has a meaning. It doesn't take the place of prayer, but it is a prayer on a capacity that overrides my words because my words are never adequate enough. But when I praise God with my flags, I have the ability to feel like and literally in a spiritual sense to be right before Him. He is my audience of one. He is the only one whose attention I am trying to get at that moment and I always come away with a clarity of who I am.

"I come away with a more defined purpose of - about my life. I come away with a joy just that to know that I have the capacity to honor Him, thank Him and be a blessing to Him and perhaps to others in that capacity. My worship is also my way of teaching, impacting that capacity to others the ability to creatively express themselves to their King, to the God they love as well from dance to being just being outside in the stillness. It's truly consolidated. It's an expression of the deepest places in my heart, to say thank you to the Lord. I am privileged, truly grateful that God brought forth this gift from me. Because it is truly one of the primary things from my life where God and God alone gets all the credit, gets all the glory, gets all the honor, and gets my all of my all."

Chapter 2

Is Flagging Scriptural?

Yes, flagging has been done for centuries. The flaggers went before the armies in the Old Testament.

In the Bible, the word referring to a flag is "standard" or "banner." The Hebrew word for flag or banner is *degel*, meaning to carry or set up a standard or banner; the NASB translation is "an army with banners." We find in Exodus 17:15 NLT: *"Moses built an altar there and named it Yahweh-Nissi (which means 'the Lord is my banner')*. Ps 60:4 NLT states, *"But you have raised up a banner for those who fear you - a rallying point in the face of attack."*

The dictionary meaning of 'banner' is "a piece of cloth bearing a design, motto, slogan, etc., sometimes attached to a staff and used as a battle standard, a flag."[6]

The word 'banner' used in the Bible refers to flags carried by the tribes with identifying emblems, or a stationary flag erected on a lofty place or mountain which, as soon as it was seen, the trumpets were blown. When God sets up a banner, He imports His Presence and protection and He extends aid to His people. He is our rallying point.

The word "standard" is defined as a level of quality or attainment; a military or ceremonial flag lifted on a pole or hoisted on a rope (flag, banner, ensign, pennant, streamer).[7]

In Num 2:2 NLT:

> "When the Israelites set up camp, each tribe will be assigned its own area. The tribal divisions will camp beneath their family banners on all four sides of the Tabernacle but at some distance from it."

We find them using the banners to mark their tribal divisions around the Tabernacle where they camped.

We still do this today; every country has its own significant flag; our military divisions have their own flags. When I was with a youth group at a large youth rally in Denver, CO, we used the America flag as a focal point to know where our group was. If we got separated from the group, we would just look for the flag, and we were able to find our way back. We look to our Stars and Stripes as a representation of our nation, just as each tribe had a flag representing them. There were 12 different flags or banners for the 12 tribes of Israel (Num 1:52, 2:2-3, 10, 18, 25, 10:14, 18, 22, 25).

In Numbers 10:14, 18, 22, 25 we find Judah's, Reuben's, Ephraim's and Dan's troops marching behind their banners. In Ps 20:5 NLT:

> "May we shout for joy when we hear of your victory and raise a victory banner in the name of our God. May the Lord answer all your prayers."

We raise victory banners to our God, marching with Him, fighting battles in the name of Jesus. He is our victory, we fight from victory, not to victory. Because Jesus has conquered, we can keep our victory banners held high. They mark who we are, stating who goes there.

In the Song of Solomon 6:4,10, we find banners of love and protection. Song of Solomon 6:4 NLT:

> "You are beautiful, my darling, like the lovely city of Tirzah. Yes, as beautiful as Jerusalem, as majestic as an army with billowing banners."

Song of Solomon 6:10 NLT:

"Who is this, arising like the dawn, as fair as the moon, as bright as the sun, as majestic as an army with billowing banners?"

In Is 11:12 *NLT:*

"He will raise a flag among the nations and assemble the exiles of Israel. He will gather the scattered people of Judah from the ends of the earth."

Is 13:2 NLT:

"Raise a signal flag on a bare hilltop. Call up an army against Babylon. Wave your hand to encourage them as they march into the palaces of the high and mighty."

Jer 50:2 NLT:

"This is what the Lord says: 'Tell the whole world and keep nothing back. Raise a signal flag to tell everyone that Babylon will fall! Her images and idols will be shattered. Her gods Bel and Marduk will be utterly disgraced.'"

As He had them do, we can do as well. We can raise our flags of worship, drawing people into worship and into His Presence, proclaiming Him to the whole world, glorifying Him, and the idols will fall.

We are to minister to the Lord Himself, in His actual presence, just as they did in King David's Tent of the Ark of the Lord. They didn't sacrifice animals in there; they gave sacrificial offerings of praise. They didn't do songs about Him; they sang to Him. We don't flag to bring glory to ourselves. We flag to bring glory to Him, to worship Him, to give Him honor, and to draw people unto Him, into His Presence where they are changed.

King David's tabernacle was not in a building but in a

tent in Jerusalem, the place where the Ark of the Covenant resided. In 1 Chronicles 16:4 NLT:

> *"David appointed the following Levites to lead the people in worship before the Ark of the Lord-to invoke His blessings, to give thanks, and to praise the Lord, the God of Israel."*

People could see the glorious light of His Presence in the Tent of the Ark of the Covenant. They weren't shut out of the Presence like in Solomon's Tabernacle, where the Ark of the Covenant was enclosed in the Holy of Holies, where a priest could enter only once a year. Now the symbol of His Presence and promise was with them. This is symbolic of the covenant we have with the Lord today as believers. He doesn't live in a "physical" tent made from animal skins or cloth but His tent is our spirit where He lives on the inside of us. We have become the Tent of the Ark of the Covenant of the Lord. He now spiritually resides in our spirit, totally filling our spirits with His Presence by the Holy Spirit. We worship Him out of our spirits.

1 Chronicles 16:7-36 NLT contains the song of thanksgiving by David when ministering to the Lord. After the Ark of the Covenant had been placed into the tent prepared for it:

> *"On that day David gave to Asaph and his fellow*
> *Levites this song of thanksgiving to the Lord:*
> *Give thanks to the Lord and proclaim his greatness.*
> *Let the whole world know what he has done.*
> *Sing to him; yes, sing his praises.*
> *Tell everyone about his wonderful deeds.*
> *Exult in his holy name;*
> *rejoice, you who worship the Lord.*
> *Search for the Lord and for his strength;*
> *continually seek him.*
> *Remember the wonders he has performed,*
> *his miracles, and the rulings he has given,*
> *you children of his servant Israel,*

Chapter 2: Is Flagging Scriptural?

you descendants of Jacob, his chosen ones.
He is the Lord our God.
His justice is seen throughout the land.
Remember his covenant forever—
the commitment he made to a thousand generations.
This is the covenant he made with Abraham
and the oath he swore to Isaac.
He confirmed it to Jacob as a decree,
and to the people of Israel as a never-ending covenant:
'I will give you the land of Canaan as your special possession.'
He said this when you were few in number,
a tiny group of strangers in Canaan.
They wandered from nation to nation,
from one kingdom to another.
Yet he did not let anyone oppress them.
He warned kings on their behalf:
'Do not touch my chosen people
and do not hurt my prophets.'
Let the whole earth sing to the Lord!
Each day proclaim the good news that he saves.
Publish his glorious deeds among the nations.
Tell everyone about the amazing things he does.
Great is the Lord!
He is most worthy of praise!
He is to be feared above all gods.
The gods of other nations are mere idols,
but the Lord made the heavens!
Honor and majesty surround him;
strength and joy fill his dwelling.
O nations of the world, recognize the Lord,
recognize that the Lord is glorious and strong.
Give to the Lord the glory he deserves!
Bring your offering and come into his presence.
Worship the Lord in all his holy splendor.
Let all the earth tremble before him.
The world stands firm and cannot be shaken.

Let the heavens be glad, and the earth rejoice!
Tell all the nations, 'The Lord reigns!'
Let the sea and everything in it shout his praise!
Let the fields and their crops burst out with joy!
Let the trees of the forest sing for joy before the Lord,
  for he is coming to judge the earth.
Give thanks to the Lord, for he is good!
  His faithful love endures forever.
Cry out, 'Save us, O God of our salvation!
Gather and rescue us from among the nations,
  so we can thank your holy name
  and rejoice and praise you.'
Praise the Lord, the God of Israel,
who lives from everlasting to everlasting!
And all the people shouted 'Amen!' and praised the Lord."

Use your flags to praise the Lord just as David sang and danced before Him.

This Tent of the Ark of the Covenant of the Lord remained in use till Solomon's Temple was built and dedicated. The Lord doesn't like to be kept in a "box." He wants to be among the people, just as He was in the tent. He wasn't locked into the Holies of Holies; He was "free" among the people, where even the Gentiles could experience Him. They could see the light of the Presence shining under the tent posts and through the legs of the priests and Levites as they worshipped around the Tent. What an awesome sight that must have been for those who listened and watched what took place, and it ministered to them. This also happens as we minister unto the Lord when we worship with our flags, honoring His Presence, bringing His Presence into the natural realm. In that Presence, people get healed and set free. The Lord has actually had me flag over people for healing. What a privilege it is to be able to minister the Presence of Him who loves us and died for us, to those who are present, while we are loving on Him.

Chapter 3

Our Authority

One of the things that it is important to know as believers and flaggers is your authority in Christ. We have been given the authority to use His Name, Jesus. We are His ambassadors in the earth today. Jesus has been given ALL authority in the earth, and He gave us His name to use. In Matthew 28 NLT, starting in verse 16:

> "Then the eleven disciples left for Galilee, going to the mountain where Jesus had told them to go. When they saw Him, they worshipped Him-but some of them doubted! Jesus came and told His disciples, 'I have been given all authority in heaven and on earth. Therefore, go and make disciples of all the nations, baptizing them in the name of the Father and the Son and the Holy Spirit. Teach these new disciples to obey all the commands I have given you. And be sure of this: I am with you always, even to the end of the age.'"

In Mark 18, beginning in verse 15 NLT:

> "And then He told them, 'Go into all the world and preach the Good News to everyone. Anyone who believes and is baptized will be saved. But anyone who refuses to believe will be condemned. These miraculous signs will accompany those who believe.

> *They will cast out demons in my name, and they will speak in new languages. They will be able to handle snakes with safety, and if they drink anything poisonous, it won't hurt them. They will be able to place their hands on the sick, and they will be healed.' When the Lord Jesus had finished talking with them, He was taken up into heaven and sat down in the place of honor at God's right hand. And the disciples went everywhere and preached, and the Lord worked through them, confirming what they said by many miraculous signs."*

In Luke in chapter 24, when Jesus appears to the disciples, beginning in verse 24 NLT:

> "Then He said, 'When I was with you before, I told you that everything written about me in the law of Moses and the prophets and the Psalms must be fulfilled.' Then He opened their minds to understand the Scriptures. And He said, 'Yes, it was written long ago that the Messiah would suffer and die and rise from the dead on the third day. It was also written that this message would be proclaimed in the authority of His name to all the nations, beginning in Jerusalem: 'There is forgiveness of sins for all who repent.' You are witnesses of all these things. And now I will send the Holy Spirit, just as My Father promised. But stay here in the city until the Holy Spirit comes and fills you with power from heaven.'"

After Jesus spoke to them, He ascended to His Father in heaven and is now seated at His right hand. In Luke 24:52 NLT:

> "So they worshiped Him and then returned to Jerusalem filled with great joy. And they spent all of their time in the Temple, praising God."

Note that they spent all of their time in the Temple,

praising God. They were continually worshiping Him, acknowledging Him, preparing for when the Holy Spirit would come on them in power at Pentecost, Acts 2.

When did God, Elohim, creator of the universe, first give authority in the earth to mankind? For that, we must return to the beginning, Genesis 1:1-2 NLT (comments in brackets are my additions):

> "In the beginning, God [Elohim, creator of the universe] created the heavens and the earth. The earth was formless and empty, and darkness covered the deep waters. And the Spirit of God [Elohim, creator of the universe] was hovering over the surface of the waters."

Here we have the earth, formless, empty, dark—no life and no light. But the Spirit of God was hovering over it, just waiting for the command so He could act.

And in verse 3 we see He, the Holy Spirit, gets His opportunity. Gen 1:3-5:

> "Then God [Elohim, creator of the universe] said, 'Let there be light,' and there was light. And God [Elohim, creator of the universe] saw that the light was good. Then He separated the light from the darkness. God [Elohim, creator of the universe] called the light 'day' and the darkness 'night.' And evening passed and morning came, marking the first day."

When God [Elohim, creator of the universe] speaks, light appears in the earth. When God said "Light Be!," light was. God put Himself back into the earth. We don't get the sun, moon and the stars until the 4th day. Verses 14-19:

> "Then God [Elohim, creator of the universe] said, 'Let lights appear in the sky to separate the day from the night. Let them be signs to mark the seasons, days

and years. Let these lights in the sky shine down on the earth.' And that is what happened. God made two great lights- the larger one to govern the day, and the smaller one to govern the night. He also made the stars. God [Elohim, creator of heaven and earth] set these lights in the sky to light the earth, to govern the day and night, and to separate the light from the darkness. And God [Elohim, creator of the universe] saw that it was good. And evening passed and morning came, marking the fourth day."

When God spoke, the action of the Holy Spirit was activated. God put Himself, who is light (1 John 1:5), back into the earth. He didn't put the natural light into the earth until the 4th day, but He put Himself back into the earth on the first day, bringing order out of chaos. And the Holy Spirit, who was hovering over this dark chaotic earth, was there just waiting for the word to be spoken so He could go to work. Words have power. Jesus was also present in the beginning, He is a co-creator of all things. In John 1:1-5 NLT:

"In the beginning the Word already existed. The Word was with God, and the Word was God. He existed in the beginning with God. God created everything through Him, and nothing was created except through Him. The Word gave life to everything that was created, and His brought light to everyone. The light shines in the darkness, and the darkness can never extinguish it."

And in Colossians 1:15-16:

"Christ is the visible image of the invisible God. He existed before anything was created and is supreme over all creation, for through the Son everything was created, both in the heavenly realm and on the earth, all that is seen and all that is unseen. Every

seat of power, realm of government, principality, and authority—it was all created through Him and for His purpose!"

This tells us that Jesus is the co-creator. So we have the Trinity working together at creation.

Man was created on the sixth day, the earth being prepared first for him. He had light, food, and water. Animals were present along with the birds, fish, all kinds of creatures for his enjoyment. The Father, in His infinite wisdom, prepared everything first; otherwise, if He had made man first before the plants and animals, Adam would not have had anything to eat. He would have needed to be continually jumping out of the way as trees popped up or animals appeared. No, The Father, Elohim, created everything Adam would need before He created him. He prepared a perfectly wonderful place for His creation.

So, now let's jump over to verse 26 in Genesis 1:

"Then God [Elohim, creator of the universe] **said, 'Let us make man in our image, to be like us. They will reign over the fish in the sea, the birds in the sky, the livestock, all the wild animals on the earth, and the smaller animals that scurry along the ground.' So God** [Elohim, creator of the universe] **created human beings in His own image. In the image of God He created them; male and female He created them. Then God** [Elohim, creator of the universe] **blessed them and said, 'Be fruitful and multiply. Fill the earth and govern it. Reign over the fish in the sea, the birds in the sky, and all the animals that scurry along the ground.' Then God** [Elohim, creator of the universe] **said, 'Look! I have given you every seed-bearing plant throughout the earth and all the fruit trees for your food. And I have given every green plant as food for all the wild animals, the birds of the sky, and the small**

animals that scurry along the ground-everything that has life.' And that is what happened. Then God [Elohim, creator of the universe] looked over all He had made, and He saw that it was very good! And evening passed and morning came, marking the sixth day."

God created man in His own image and after His likeness; we look like Him and we can act like Him, we have His character built into us. We are equal with the Holy Spirit (not equal to, but equal with). **He gave man dominion over everything on the earth.** It was to be under our control through Him. Now we work alongside the Lord as co-laborers through us, through our words to get things done here on earth. He reveals to us what He wants done, we pray and speak it forth, and He carries it out. He is sovereign, which means nothing rules over Him, but He gave dominion of the earth to mankind. Psalm 8 confirms this (NLT):

"O Lord, our Lord, your majestic name fills the earth! Your glory is higher than the heavens. You have taught children and infants to tell of your strength, silencing your enemies and all who oppose you. When I look at the night sky and see the work of your fingers - the moon and the stars you set in place - what are mere mortals that you should think about them, human beings that you should care for them? **Yet you made them only a little lower than God** [Elohim, creator of the universe] **and crowned them with glory and honor. You gave them charge of everything you made, putting all things under their authority-the flocks and the herds and all the wild animals, the birds in the sky, the fish in the sea, and everything that swims the ocean currents.** *O Lord, our Lord, your majestic name fills the earth!"*

Chapter 3: Our Authority

We were given authority over the earth, but what happened? How was it lost? Adam gave it to satan, by his disobedience. Now, instead of God working through man, satan is working through man. God is still sovereign, no one rules over Him, but now man has a new headship, satan, who is called the Prince of the Power of the air.

So where did this happen? In the garden. In Gen 2:15-17:

"The LORD God [Jehovah, provider, Elohim, creator of the universe] placed man in the Garden of Eden to tend and watch over it. But the LORD God [Jehovah, provider, Elohim, creator of the universe] warned him, 'you may freely eat the fruit of every tree in the garden - except the tree of the knowledge of good and evil. If you eat its fruit, you are sure to die.'"

The Father warns Adam; He gave him a limitation to test his obedience to Him. They were created in the image and likeness of God, functioning in His glory. He had placed His spirit within them; in the Hebrew, it says they were speaking spirits (Gen 2:7). In verse 2:15, He gave them the job to tend and watch over the garden. That was their job. Adam was to teach Eve, for she was created from him; she hadn't heard the words of instruction that the LORD gave to Adam when He created him.

The Father creates the woman, Eve, from Adam. In chapter 3 of Genesis, we find satan coming in and deceiving them by his words. Adam, who had dominion over satan in the garden, should not have allowed him to be there or have conversations with him. So continuing in chapter 3 verse 1:

"The serpent was the shrewdest of all the wild animals the Lord God [Jehovah, provider, Elohim, creator of the universe] had made. One day he asked the woman, 'Did God really say you must not eat the fruit from any of the trees in the garden?' 'Of

course we may eat from the trees in the garden,' the woman replied. 'It's only the fruit from the tree in the middle of the garden that we are not allowed to eat. God said, "You must not eat it or even touch it; if you do, you will die."' 'You won't die!' the serpent replied to the woman. 'God knows that your eyes will be opened as soon as you eat it, and you will be like God, knowing both good and evil.' The woman was convinced. She saw the tree was beautiful and its fruit looked delicious, and she wanted the wisdom it would give her. So she took some of the fruit and ate it. Then she gave some to her husband, who was with her, and he ate it. At that moment their eyes were opened, and they suddenly felt shame at their nakedness."

Satan was introducing doubt to them, for they were already like God, created in His image and likeness. The Holy Spirit was living on the inside of them and they were living out of His glory. But satan deceived Eve, and Adam sinned. They allowed their physical senses to have influence over them. They did not keep their bodies and physical senses under the control of their spirit, which contained the Holy Spirit. Satan, by his words, affected their souls, speaking to their minds and emotions. He was speaking fear into their lives, by introducing thoughts that they were not like God. Eve also added to what the LORD had told Adam. The LORD never said that they couldn't touch the tree, they were only not supposed to eat from it. They added to the requirement; this is what man and religion do. Man and religion add requirements to what God has told us to do, making living for Him more difficult. When they by-passed their spirit, listened to their carnal nature, and ate of the fruit of the tree of good and evil, they spiritually died. They lost the glory and now saw their nakedness and felt ashamed. Satan got what he wanted—dominion in the earth. He had gotten kicked out of heaven because he wanted to be above God and he hated man. Satan had fellowship with the LORD which he lost due to his disobedience and pride; but now, he got what man had, what he was after—dominion.

So how did man get dominion back? Through Jesus! The Word/Jesus became flesh and dwelt among us. Jesus had to take on flesh to redeem man, for to live on this earth you must have a physical body. It was a man who broke covenant with God, not God with man, so Jesus had to come as a man to redeem man. This plan had been established from the foundation of the world; God, in His infinite knowledge and mercy, knew that by giving man free choice he would ultimately screw up. So He had the PLAN! Satan never knew about this PLAN, but he knew by the words spoken to him in the garden that a man would come and smash his head; He just didn't know who. If satan had known, he never would have gotten Jesus crucified, but that too was part of the Father's PLAN. So, we have Jesus coming as a baby (who satan tried to kill), growing up, doing ministry, healing the sick, freeing people from demonic strongholds, setting the captives free, and starting His own worldwide ministry. He suffered excruciating pain, a horrendous death on the cross, goes to hell and is further tormented there. But the Father, through the power of the Holy Spirit, raised Jesus from the dead, conquering hell, the grave, and all sickness and disease. All of that being left in the pit of hell. Jesus, through His perfect obedience here on the earth, won us back dominion, and we now have that dominion by using His name. When we understand and use our authority as a believer in the finished work of Jesus Christ, we, in essence, are worshipping Him. We are giving Him honor and reverence by acknowledging the work He did for us on this earth.

So when you have "storms" in your life, you can take dominion over them. Just as Jesus spoke to the storm in Mark 4:35-41, you can speak to storms in your life through the use of the name of Jesus. Let's look at that story beginning in verse 35:

> *"As evening came, Jesus said to his disciples, 'Let's cross to the other side of the lake.' So they took Jesus in the boat and started out, leaving the crowds behind (although other boats followed). But soon a fierce storm came up. High waves were breaking into the boat, and it began to fill with water. Jesus was sleeping at the back of the boat with His head on a cushion. The disciples woke Him up, shouting, 'Teacher, don't you care that we're going to drown?' When Jesus woke up, He rebuked the wind and said to the waves, 'Silence! Be still!' Suddenly the wind stopped, and there was a great calm. Then He asked them, 'Why are you afraid? Do you still have no faith?' The disciples were absolutely terrified. 'Who is this man?' they asked each other. 'Even the wind and waves obey Him!'"*

Jesus had just spent many hours teaching them about the principles of the Kingdom, but they really weren't getting it. How many times has that happened to us?

Think about this, Jesus had spent a long day teaching them important kingdom concepts, and He grew tired. As it tells us in verse 35, "As evening came Jesus said to His disciples, 'Let's cross over to the other side of the lake.'" Jesus is still on a mission to free the demon-possessed man and He goes to sleep on a cushion in the back of the boat. Jesus is not fearful, He is walking in His Father's will, so He takes a nap on their way across the lake. But suddenly a fierce storm comes up. Imagine that. Jesus is on His way to free the demon-possessed man and a fierce storm comes up to try to stop Him. Who do you think is behind that storm? Satan, of course. He doesn't want that man free, for he, the demon-possessed man, was causing great havoc in that area. So here comes the storm. Jesus isn't afraid; He is greater than the storm and He is greater than satan. But who is afraid? The disciples, because they still don't really understand whom they have with them. He has already demonstrated miracle after miracle, but just like us sometimes, we don't always get it. We don't realize whom we have with us. The disciples had Jesus, creator of the universe, physically in the boat with them, and they were afraid. We, as born again Christians, have the Spirit of Jesus, the Holy Spirit, spiritually residing on the inside of us, and how many times are we afraid?

So, here they have the creator of the world in the boat with them, and they are afraid. The water is coming in; don't you think Jesus knew what was happening? He is probably getting wet, too. But I think He wanted to see what they were going to do. They were terrified, and what happens sometimes when you are terrified in a situation? "Brain freeze." Emotions have taken over; they do not remember what He has taught them. So they wake Jesus, shouting at Him, "Don't you care we are going to drown?" Does Jesus shake in His "boots" wondering, "Oh, my, what are we going to do?" No, He rebukes the storm saying, "Silence, be still!" He knew who He was and His authority; He had faith!

When Jesus had sent them out two by two, He had told them, *"Look, I have given you authority over all the power of the enemy, and you can walk among snakes and scorpions and crush them. Nothing will injure you"* (Luke 10:19). Just as Jesus had given them the power over the enemy, He gave you that same authority when you took Him as Lord of your life. It is one of our benefits. For we now have the creator of the universe living on the inside of us in our spirit. So when you get into a storm in your life, and we all have many, we can use the name of Jesus to change the situation. I use it a lot in storms; I call the weather as I want it to be. In Jesus' name, I tell satan he can't bring any tornadoes (which are just swirling demons out to cause destruction), destructive lightning, hail, torrential rain, or destructive or ground line winds. If we need rain, I say you can just allow rain to come. I will look at the weather radar and declare what I want to see. I call storms to dissipate, cease. It is much easier to take authority over the weather if it is not already upon you. But I do call hail to stop if it is already upon us and I didn't know ahead of time it was predicted. I call adequate rainfall for our summers, a long warm fall, mild winters with adequate snow coverage. You want a nice day for an event, call it in, but I also try to take into consideration what the farmers need for the weather. If rain is predicted and we are in need of a shower, I let it come. I will say to the Lord, my rain barrels are empty, please fill them.

As you "practice" on smaller situations, you will build up your faith, and as you build up your faith in your words, your authority will increase; you will see greater results. Watch what you say, don't say what you don't mean, or your words won't mean anything, and the devil will not listen to you. Also, remember to walk in love as Jesus commanded. Be like Jesus, John 5:19. He only did what He saw His Father do and said what He heard His Father say. As you learn this, you will see more victories in your life when you pray and when you flag. Because the colors in your flag speak, do you believe what it says? I once was in a church where I discerned a demonic spirit residing; all I had to do was take out my triple white flag—representing purity, holiness, and the Bride of Christ—out of my bag, and it left. I didn't even have to wave it; I only took it out. Why? Because that entity knew that I knew who I was in Christ, and he was had. Worship with your flags, honoring the LORD, using your authority, helping to keep your homes free, neighborhoods free, and churches free of demonic entities. Bring in peace; that is what Jesus did in the storm, He said, "Peace, be still!" Call that peace into the storms in your life, too.

Something that is really important in using your authority

is you can't use it against people. If you try to manipulate people using your authority, that is witchcraft. What did Jesus tell the disciples when He sent them out? *"Look I have given you authority over all the power of the enemy."* You may think and feel a person is your enemy, but your real enemy is the demonic entity behind and influencing that person. Take authority over it, not over the person.

You primarily have authority only over the area where you live; it is called habitational authority. I can only take authority over the weather where I live. I can't take authority over the weather on the east coast when I live in NW Wisconsin. I have taken authority over where my siblings live because they are part of me. I do this for my children as well. I can intercede for people on the east coast about the weather, but I can't take direct authority over it. I can, however, if someone who lives there gives me that authority or if the Lord has expanded my authority in Him.

We listened to an audio teaching by Terry Mize on authority. He told the story of how he would pray over his mother-in-law when she was sick, for she had given him that authority. But then she got married a second time, and she transferred that authority over to her new husband. The problem was he didn't know his authority and how to use it. He didn't know how to use his authority over sickness to get her well when she got sick. One time when Terry and his wife were out of town (before the days of cell phones), they came back to their hotel room one evening, and the button on the phone was blinking indicating they had a message. So they get the message, telling them they needed to call home immediately. But by the time they were able to call home, Terry's mother-in-law had died. Terry said he was quite angry with God, asking Him why did this happen? It was because her husband didn't know his authority, and Terry no longer had it. For she had transferred it to her husband when they married. She had also quit calling them when she was sick to ask for prayer, so they didn't even know that she was ill when they had left town to go to the conference. Tragic!

We can take authority over things in our children's lives when they are smaller and live in our homes. But once they leave and they don't give that to you, you no longer have that authority. You can still pray for them, interceding on their behalf, but you don't have authority over the demonic that may be working in their lives. He taught that if you try to raise someone from the dead, and the family hasn't given you authority to do so, it won't work. Or it won't work to go to a hospital and try praying over everyone; you don't have authority there. That is a reason why we sometimes don't see our prayers answered, and we get frustrated.[8]

Here is another story on authority: my husband and I were taking care of a neighbor's home while they were gone to Arizona for part of the winter. We would shovel snow, feed the birds, and water the plants. Just keeping a general eye on the place. Because we had been asked to take care of their house, we had authority in it. Well, the lady of the house had a stuffed figure of a witch doctor hanging on her wall, and one day it "spoke" to me. I function in the discerning of spirits at times. So after I got home that day I called her and said her witch doctor had spoken to me. She just said, "What, what do you mean it spoke to you?" She knew of my stories of going to Montana with another friend (I had gone with this friend to help move her parents back to Montana. On that trip, the Lord taught us both how to discern a demonic presence in things—pictures, carvings, beds, chairs, anything). The stuffed figure was nasty, and I didn't want to go there while it hung on the wall, so I asked her if I could take it down. She agreed to that. I couldn't get it clean of the demonic entity on it; I didn't have the authority, but she did let me take it off the wall so I would continue taking care of her house. So the next time we went, I took a small box to put it in. I anointed it and put it in the box, taped the box shut and anointed the outside of the box. This way the demonic spirit was trapped in the box, in the figure, and couldn't get out to harass me. So in this case, I couldn't remove the demonic entity on the figure but I could "lock" it in the box. Sometimes you can get items clean, but there are times when they need to be burnt or destroyed.

So as we continually learn who we are in Christ, where our authority lies, worshipping Him, knowing the benefits of our salvation, we will have a greater effect for His Kingdom in our world. Remember as we co-labor with Him, participating with the Holy Spirit, we help to bring glory to God here in this realm.

Chapter 4

The Blessing

What is The Blessing? The empowerment to be fruitful, to produce in all realms of life. When God prayed over Adam, after He created him, He conferred The Blessing upon him (Genesis 1:28: *"Then God blessed them and said, 'Be fruitful and multiply. Fill the earth and govern it. Reign over the fish in the sea, the birds in the sky, and all the animals that scurry along the ground'"*). He again conferred The Blessing on Noah and his family when they left the Ark.

We have the Blessing by what Jesus did when He conquered hell and the grave. Through His complete and perfect obedience to His Father, He fulfilled the PLAN of redemption, having been put into place before the foundation of the world. Let's look at what Paul the apostle had to say about this in Ephesians. Ephesians 1:3-6 NLT:

> *"All praise to God [Elohim, creator of the universe], the Father of our Lord [Master] Jesus Christ [the anointed one and His anointing], who has blessed us with every spiritual blessing in the heavenly realms because we are united with Christ [the anointed one and His anointing]. Even before He made the world, God [Elohim, creator of the universe] loved us and chose us in Christ [the anointed one and*

His anointing] to be holy and without fault in His eyes. **God** [Elohim, creator of the universe] **decided in advance to adopt us into His own family by bringing us to Himself through Jesus Christ. This is what He wanted to do, and it gave Him great pleasure.** *So we praise God* [Elohim, creator of the universe] *for the glorious grace that He poured out on us who belong to His dear Son."*

Do you see that? What He did? Before He even made the world, He loved us, He blessed us in Christ to be holy and without fault in His eyes. How? By the perfect work of redemption, by the shedding of Jesus' most precious blood. Why? Because of His love for mankind, for mankind that was created in His image and likeness. Why did He plan to redeem us? Why did He even bother? Why didn't He just destroy man when man sinned? Because if He had destroyed us, it would have been like He was destroying Himself, for He made us like Himself.

Can you grasp that, that He chose us to be holy and without fault in His eyes? How? How can we be without fault in His eyes? For surely not by what we do, for our work is like filthy rags. No, by what Jesus did! By His suffering and death, by the shedding of His most precious blood. Every drop of blood was shed for us. Every single drop of His blood was an explosion of His love for us. Grasp that!

His skin and muscles were ripped to shreds, hardly an inch of skin was left on His body, for that is what it says in Is 52:14 NLT:

> *"But many were amazed when they saw him. His face was so disfigured He seemed hardly human, and from His appearance, one would scarcely know He was a man."*

He did this because of His great love for us! That all-encompassing, surpassing love, not dependent on what we do, only on what He did. Do you know this gave Him great pleasure? Selah! Think on that!

God adopted us into His family by bringing us to Himself through Jesus, His son, by His great, unequaled suffering. When Jesus came, He knew He would have to go through this, the beatings, mockings, and crucifixion. But it gave Him great pleasure. He knew the joy of the ending; it gave Him strength to persevere through all the pain and suffering. He knew His Father would never forsake Him to hell and the grave; He knew He would rise again on the third day. He knew He would beat satan and conquer him, taking captives captive. HE KNEW! Do you know?

Do you know that in Eph 1:7 NLT:

> *"That He is so rich in kindness and grace, that He purchased our freedom with the blood of His Son and forgave our sins? He showered His kindness on us, along with all wisdom and understanding."?*

Do you know He has forgiven all your sins past, present, and future? All of them, if you have taken Jesus as Lord of your life, He has forgiven them all, and He remembers them no more. If He doesn't remember them, neither should you. Do you know that this God [Elohim, creator of the universe] lives on the inside of you? He took up residence when you took Jesus as Lord of your life. He took up permanent residence in your spirit. That is such an awesome thought that the creator of everything, everything around you, that creator lives on the inside of you 24/7. You don't have to knock on the doors of heaven to get His attention, or on the glass floor of heaven. No, He is within you. Just speak to Him there. All wisdom and understanding are there in your spirit by the Holy Spirit. Just seek it out. **We are equal with the Holy Spirit** (not to, but with) for the Holy Spirit is greater, more powerful than us. When we are born again, He fills up our spirit with Himself, making us one with Him, thereby making us equal with Him but not equal to

Him. It is Him in us that helps us to do all the things we are called to do.

Let's continue looking in verse 9-11 of Ephesians chapter 1 NLT:

> *"God has now revealed to us His mysterious will regarding Him, which is to fulfill His own good plan. And this is the plan: At the right time, He will bring everything together under the authority of Christ [the anointed one and His anointing] in heaven and on earth. Furthermore, because we are united with Christ [the anointed one and His anointing], we have received an inheritance from God, for He chose us in advance, and He makes everything work out according to His plan."*

God [Elohim, creator of the universe] makes everything work out according to HIS PLAN! At the right time, He brought everything under the authority of Jesus, everything in heaven and on earth, and He gave us back that authority through the name of Jesus. He restored what Adam gave away to satan in the Garden.

Now, what do we do with that authority? Let's see what Jesus said one night when He was eating with his disciples, and He tells them this:

> *"Anyone who believes in me will do the same works I have done, and even greater works because I am going to be with the Father"* (John 14:12 NLT).

Come on, really Jesus, we are going to do what You have done? Heal the sick, raise the dead, cast out demons? Really? Yes, really! Isn't this what Jesus told them in Matt 28:18-20?

> *"I have been given all authority in heaven and on earth. Therefore, go and make disciples of all the nations, baptizing them in the name of the Father and the Son and Holy Spirit. Teach these new*

disciples to obey all the commandments I have given you. **And be sure of this: I am with you always, even to the end of the age.**"

Mark 16:15-18:

"And then He told them (just before He ascended into heaven) 'Go into all the world and preach the Good News/Gospel to everyone. Anyone who believes and is baptized will be saved. But anyone who refuses to believe will be condemned. These miraculous signs will accompany those who believe: They will cast out demons in My name, and they will speak in new languages. They will be able to handle poisonous snakes with safety, and if they drink anything poisonous, it won't hurt them. They will be able to place their hands on the sick, and they will be healed.'"

Now, we do that with the authority that He commanded us to do—heal the sick, cast out demons, set the captives free, preach the Gospel, the Good News. Make disciples of all the nations. Raise the dead! That can be taken more than one way—raise the dead. Raise the physical dead, and the spiritually dead, those who haven't given their lives over to Jesus. That could be someone who has never heard the Good News or someone who thinks they are saved but aren't; they have just been living a dead religion. Both need the Good News preached to them to get them healed, set free, and saved!

Where do we do this "work" from? Where is Jesus now? Let's look again in the first chapter of Ephesians, starting in verse 19, Paul is praying:

"I also pray that you will understand the incredible greatness of God's power for us who believe Him. This is **the same mighty power that raised Christ from the dead and seated him in the place of**

honor at God's right hand in the heavenly realms. Now He is far above any ruler or authority or power or leader or anything else not only in this world but also in the world to come. God has put all things under the authority of Christ and has made him head over all things for the benefit of the church. And the church (us) *is His body; it is made full and complete by Christ, who fills all things everywhere with Himself."*

Where is Jesus now? Seated at the right hand of the Father in heaven. Where are we if we have taken Jesus as Lord of our lives? IN HIM! His Spirit, the Holy Spirit lives on the inside of us, so we are in Him, seated at the right hand of the Father in heaven. This is where we function from, from victory in Him. He is the head of the body and we are the body, the church. We are connected! We co-labor with Him. If He has authority over all things and He is the head, and if we are part of Him, the body, we also have authority over all things in Him. And we use that authority in His name to get people healed, delivered and set free. We don't do it in our power and authority; we do it in Him by the power of the Holy Spirit. This is what the gospel of Grace/the Good News is all about. Grace is Jesus, the Good News who came to set us free. We get the Holy Spirit living in our spirit when we become saved, and we receive greater power when we receive the Baptism of the Holy Spirit upon us. The Holy Spirit is in us for us, but upon us for somebody else.

How do we get that greater power of the Holy Spirit? I will talk about it in the next chapter on the Baptism of the Holy Spirit, a necessity for all believers, a free gift from the Father, given to all the disciples at Pentecost. It wasn't just for the early church; it is just as important for us now. It is what Jesus received at His baptism in the Jordan River. If He needed it to minister, so do we! The Baptism of the Holy Spirit helps us to hear and move in the things of the

Spirit better; this is important in flagging as well. It helps us function for Him, make flags and do in this world what He wants to be done.

Chapter 5

The Baptism of the Holy Spirit

Jesus, at His baptism, received the Baptism of the Holy Spirit for power in ministry, He didn't need salvation first, for He had never sinned. He went from functioning in the natural realm to functioning in the supernatural realm. We must do the same. Flagging is more than just waving flags around. We need to be saved and receive the Baptism of the Holy Spirit in order to truly flow in worship to Him, bringing about what He wants to be done in the earth, and discerning what is around us properly.

In Matt 3:13-17 NLT we see Jesus being baptized by John:

> "Then Jesus went from Galilee to the Jordan River to be baptized by John. But John tried to talk Him out of it. 'I am the one who needs to be baptized by you,' he said. 'So why are you coming to me?' But Jesus said, 'It should be done, for we must carry out all that God requires.' So John agreed to baptize Him. After His baptism, as Jesus came up out of the water, the heavens were opened and he saw the Spirit of God descending like a dove and settling on Him. And a voice from heaven said, 'This is my dearly beloved Son, who brings me great joy.'"

Jesus wasn't baptized as a sign of salvation, for Jesus had never sinned. It was a baptism of the Spirit for power.

When did the disciples receive the power they needed for ministry? At Pentecost! Remember what the disciples were doing after the death of Jesus; they were hiding. John 20:19-23:

> *"That Sunday evening [after His resurrection) the disciples were meeting behind locked doors because they were afraid of the Jewish leaders. Suddenly, Jesus was standing there among them! 'Peace be with you,' He said. As He spoke, He showed them the wounds in His hands and His side. They were filled with joy when they saw the Lord! Again He said, 'Peace be with you. As the Father has sent me, so I am sending you.' Then He breathed on them and said, 'Receive the Holy Spirit. If you forgive anyone's sins, they are forgiven. If you do not forgive them, they are not forgiven.'"*

The disciples are petrified, terrified! Jesus died, but now Mary Magdalene says she has seen Him, and Peter and John have seen the empty grave clothes. They are afraid of what the Jewish leaders are going to do to them, for they killed their leader; now the disciples are hiding out. You can hide out but Jesus will find you!! So here we find Jesus coming to them as they hid behind locked doors. He says to them "Peace be with you." He shows them His hands and His side, and they realize it is HIM! They are excited He is back; now they believe it is truly Him, He has returned. Then He says to them again, *"Peace be with you. As the Father has sent me, so I am sending you."* Maybe they are thinking *where is He sending us?* They still didn't quite understand what Jesus had been telling them for three years. He then breathed on them and said, *"Receive the Holy Spirit. If you forgive anyone's sins, they are forgiven. If you do not forgive them, they are not forgiven."*

When was the first time God breathed on man? In the Garden, when God made man in His own image and likeness (Genesis 2:7):

Chapter 5: The Baptism of the Holy Spirit

"Then the LORD God formed the man from the dust of the ground. He breathed the breath of life into the man's nostrils, and the man became a living person."

God formed man out of the dirt and then He breathed His life/His Spirit into him. He created a speaking spirit, created in His image and after His likeness, having His character. Then man sinned, and he spiritually died, for God no longer was residing in his spirit. But God had a PLAN. Jesus redeemed man, He paid the price. When Jesus breathed on them in that upper room, they received His Spirit, His life back into their spirits (John 20:22). They were now born again. They became new recreated species. Their dead spirit/the old man controlled by the devil was gone and they received again the new life, the Holy Spirit of God. Now they have the Spirit of God living on the inside of them, the same Spirit that raised Jesus from the dead. Got that! **The same Spirit that raised Jesus from the dead, is now living in them.**

But they were still afraid; they were still hiding behind locked doors. John 20:24:

"One of the twelve disciples Thomas (nicknamed the Twin), was not with the others when Jesus came. They told him, 'We have seen the Lord!' But he replied, 'I won't believe it unless I see the nail wounds in His hands, put my fingers into them, and place my hand into the wound in His side.' Eight days later the disciples were together again, and this time Thomas was with them. ***The doors were locked;*** *but suddenly, as before, Jesus was standing among them."*

So where did the power come from for Peter, afraid, hiding out for fear of the Jews, to preach to 3,000 on Pentecost? They are saved, they have the Holy Spirit living on the inside of them in their spirit, but are still afraid. That power came when the Holy Spirit came **upon** them at Pentecost. Their spirits had been recreated, but not their souls (their minds, wills, and emotions). The Holy Spirit is in them for them, but He must come **upon** them for power and ministry. **Their spirits were "filled" with the Holy Spirit but now it must overflow out of them like a river for others.** You can have a bottle of water and it is "full," but it is not truly full until it overflows and runs over. They had been filled when Jesus breathed on them, but they needed to overflow and run over to affect others. We also need that continual overflow.

Let's now look at Acts 2 NLT beginning in verse 1:

"On the day of Pentecost, seven weeks after Jesus' resurrection, the believers were meeting together in one place. Suddenly, there was a sound from heaven like the roaring of a mighty windstorm in the skies above them, and He filled the house where they were meeting. ***Then, what looked like flames or tongues of fire appeared and settled on each of them.****"* [Like if someone came and sat on you and enveloped you in their arms, encompassing you]. *"And everyone present was filled with the Holy Spirit and began speaking in other languages/tongues, as the Holy Spirit gave them this ability. Godly Jews from many nations were living in Jerusalem at that time. When they heard this sound, they came running to see what it was all about, and they were bewildered to hear their own languages/tongues being spoken by the believers. They were beside themselves with wonder. 'How can this be?' they exclaimed. 'These people are all from Galilee, and yet we hear them speaking the languages of the lands where we were born!'"*

Remember in Acts 1 how Jesus had told the disciples not to leave Jerusalem until the Father sends them what He had promised. The Promise of the Father was the coming of the Holy Spirit upon them. Beginning in Acts 1:3 NLT:

Chapter 5: The Baptism of the Holy Spirit

> "During the forty days after His crucifixion, He/ Jesus appeared to the apostles from time to time and proved to them in many ways that He was actually alive. On these occasions He talked to them about the Kingdom of God. In one of these meetings as He was eating a meal with them, He told them, 'Do not leave Jerusalem until the Father sends you what He promised. Remember, I have told you about this before. John baptized with water, but in just a few days you will be baptized with the Holy Spirit. But when the Holy Spirit has **come upon** you, you will receive **power** and will tell people about me everywhere-in Jerusalem, throughout Judea, in Samaria, and to the ends of the earth.' It was not long after He said this that He was taken up into the sky while they were watching, and He disappeared into a cloud."

There are two baptisms: baptism with water and the Baptism of the Holy Spirit with fire. In the first you were cleansed and recreated; the second you are endued with power for ministry by the working of the Holy Spirit. Both are by faith in God. By faith through grace—the redeeming action of Jesus—you are born again (Grace = Jesus = **G**od's **R**edemption **A**t **C**hrist's **E**xpense). It is by the working of the Holy Spirit that the sick are healed, the captives set free, and the lost are redeemed. Not by any power of ourselves, but only by the power and workings of the Holy Spirit. The Baptism of the Holy Spirit is the gateway into the supernatural for service. This is how Jesus ministered; remember, He was baptized by the Holy Spirit at the Jordan River before He began His ministry. Even in Acts 2:38, we find this:

> "And no doubt you know that God anointed Jesus of Nazareth with the Holy Spirit and with power. Then Jesus went around doing good and healing all who were oppressed by the devil, for God was with Him."

In the Old Testament, the Holy Spirit would temporarily come upon a prophet to speak or demonstrate the power of God. He didn't permanently stay with them. But now, once you have received the Baptism of the Holy Spirit you keep Him; it is not temporary as with the Old Testament prophets.

In the times of the early church, these two baptisms happened close together. In Acts 2:14, Peter had been preaching to the crowds, and in verses *37-39:*

> *"Peter's words convicted them deeply, and they said to him and to the other apostles, 'Brothers, what shall we do?' Peter replied, 'Each of you must turn from your sins and turn to God, and be baptized in the name of Jesus Christ for the forgiveness of your sins. Then you will receive the gift of the Holy Spirit. This promise is to you and to your children, and even to the Gentiles - all who have been called by the Lord our God.'"*

Verse 43 tells us that after receiving the Baptism of the Holy Spirit, the apostles performed many miraculous signs and wonders. Before this, they were hiding out afraid; now they have received the promise of the Father, the power of the Holy Spirit. There wasn't a long duration between water baptism and the Baptism of the Holy Spirit as we find many times today. Many people have received the baptism of water but not the Baptism of the Holy Spirit for power. I was baptized as a child but I was an adult when I received the Baptism of the Holy Spirit. And I have found in my life that once I received the Baptism of the Holy Spirit, I could understand the scriptures more clearly and praying became easier, for if I didn't know what to pray, I would pray "in the spirit" with other tongues. Romans 8:26 NLT:

> *"And the Holy Spirit helps us in our weakness. For example, we don't know what God wants us to pray*

for. But the Holy Spirit prays for us with groanings that cannot be expressed in words."

If I needed understanding on a subject, I would also pray in the spirit and get understanding by the Holy Spirit, who lives now inside of me. You can pray in the spirit and ask for the interpretation in your natural tongue to understand what you have been told. Speaking in tongues is controlled by you; you start and stop speaking at your will. Once when I was building a website for the online business I had, I would pray in tongues when I got stuck and didn't know what to write. I would pray for the interpretation and write what I was given.

Praying in the Spirit, speaking in tongues is a gift of the Holy Spirit when you receive the Baptism of the Holy Spirit. It is evidence of having received it. It is what the disciples received on Pentecost, it is what the Jews heard when they said:

"Godly Jews from many nations were living in Jerusalem at that time. When they heard this sound, they came running to see what it was all about, and they were bewildered to hear their own languages/ tongues being spoken by the believers. They were beside themselves with wonder. 'How can this be?' they exclaimed. 'These people are all from Galilee, and yet we hear them speaking the languages of the lands where we were born!" (Acts 2:5-8 NLT).

God will give you a new, individual language, a language of the Holy Spirit for you to communicate with Him or the angels. No one has the same prayer language as someone else, it a special communication of the Holy Spirit through you to the Father. It is a most wonderful gift; you can pray in the spirit at any time, any place, always communicating with the Father, praying out what He wants to be prayed because it is by the Holy Spirit! 1 Cor 14:2:

"For if you have the ability to speak in tongues, you will be talking only to God, since people won't be

able to understand you. You will be speaking by the power of the Spirit, but it will all be mysterious."

The devil can't understand you, either.

We are a spirit and we are to live out of our spirit, not out of our soul and flesh. In Gal 5:16-17:

"So I advise you to live according to your new life in the Holy Spirit. Then you won't be doing what your sinful life craves. The old sinful nature loves to do evil, which is just the opposite of what the Holy Spirit wants. And the Spirit gives us desires that are the opposite of what the sinful nature desires."

We are to be led by the Holy Spirit in everything we do. It is by the Holy Spirit that we receive the gifts of the Spirit, to do as Jesus did.

Another way of looking at the Baptism of the Holy Spirit is this: when the Holy Spirit came upon them, it was like He actually engulfed them. He consumed them, for God is a consuming fire. It is if they received their own pillar of fire that would empower them and lead them throughout their lives. They each got their own "God Hug"!

When flagging, being baptized in the Holy Spirit helps you to follow the flow of the Holy Spirit, what He is doing and what He wants to be done. It helps you to flow better in worship unto the Lord. It helps you to minister in a way pleasing to Him, giving Him glory. It is essential in our service to the Lord and to others. Life changes immensely once you have the Baptism of the Holy Spirit; it is one of the greatest blessings of the Lord. You must be saved first before you received the Baptism of the Holy Spirit. You can, however, receive them consecutively, so I will add a prayer for both. If you are already saved, you only need to pray the prayer to receive the Baptism of the Holy Spirit.

Prayer of Salvation: "Father, I thank you for who You are and all that You are. I humbly submit my life to you, for it says in scripture that anyone who calls on your name will be saved (Acts 2:21). Therefore, I am calling on You and confessing with my mouth that Jesus Christ is Lord. I believe in my heart that Jesus Christ died and was buried and raised from the dead (Rom 10: 9-10). I believe He paid the full penalty for all of my sins. I repent of my sins and believe I am now in right standing with Him as a new creature (2 Cor 5:17). I thank you, Lord, for saving me. Take my life and do something with it."

To receive the Baptism of the Holy Spirit: "Father, I am Your child, I have been reborn, recreated. I am saved! As it says in Luke 11:13 NLT: *'If imperfect parents know how to lovingly take care of their children and give them what they need, how much more will the perfect heavenly Father give the Holy Spirit's fullness when his children ask him.'* I am asking You, Lord, to fill me with the Holy Spirit. By faith, I receive it right now! Fill me with Your power to live this new life, rise up within me as I praise the Lord with my mouth. Fill my mouth with Your words, with other tongues not my own as You give me utterance (Acts 2:4). Thank you, Lord, for baptizing me with Your Holy Spirit. You, Holy Spirit, are welcome in my life!"

Now with your mouth, began speaking. You have to speak, use your voice, for as you do, He will give you a supernatural language all your own to communicate with Him and angels. You have control of when and where; He doesn't force you to speak. You are not a puppet; you stop and start at your will, not His. Be blessed with this most awesome gift of the Baptism of the Holy Spirit, for it was what Jesus received at His baptism in the River Jordan. Just as He needed it for ministry, so do we. Now allow that river of life to flow out of you for others.

Chapter 6

Spirit, Soul & Body

We are three-part beings; we are a spirit, we have a soul and we live in a body. We cannot exist here without a body, our earth suit. Our souls consist of our minds, wills, emotions, conscience, and our personality; our souls and our spirits came together from heaven, "planted" into the fertilized egg at conception. They came out of the Father's heart into us. So even though our spirits have been recreated and filled with the Holy Spirit when we accepted Jesus as Lord, our souls have to be renewed or transformed into the Word of God.

We need to change what we are thinking and feeling to line up to the Word of God to live a free spirit-filled life. It doesn't happen automatically when you are born again; your spirit was recreated, you are a new species, but you still have the same soul and body. If you were short before you were born again, you will be short after you are born again. If you were fat before you will be fat after; the body is not changed when you take Jesus as Lord. We need to renew our minds and crucify or put down our flesh. We need to live out of our spirits, not letting our flesh or our souls rule over us. That is why the apostles were still afraid, hiding because they hadn't yet renewed their minds. As they prayed and remembered what the Lord had taught them over the past three years, a transformation began to take place; their minds became renewed and transformed. We also need to renew and transform our minds, wills, and emotions. We do this by reading, meditating on the Word, praying in the spirit and listening to anointed preachers.

The scriptural basis for this belief is 1 Thessalonians 5:23 NLT:

> *"Now may the God of peace make you holy in every way, and may **your whole spirit and soul and body** be kept blameless until that day when our Lord Jesus Christ comes again."*

Most Christians don't understand this. At one time, I did not either. I was raised where the spirit and soul were referred to as the same. But that is a cause for major confusion in understanding the Word of God, for we need to always rightly divide the Word of God. Our spiritual man is really who we are. When our spirits leave our bodies, we die, taking our souls with our spirits. It is our spirit that keeps us alive. If you have read any near-death experience stories, people will talk about rising up over their bodies and seeing themselves lying on an operating table or bed or wherever they were when they died. They can do this because they are a spirit looking down on their dead bodies. It is our spirit that goes to either heaven or hell when we die. We take our souls with us, our minds, wills, emotions, personality, but our bodies are made up of the elements of this earth and to it, it will return. It is the condition of our spirits, not our souls, that determines if we go to heaven or hell. If we have taken Jesus as Lord and the Holy Spirit has taken up residence in our spirits, then we go on to heaven; if not we will go to hell, a place created for the devil and his cohorts.

I heard a story about a man who had taken Jesus as Lord when he was younger, but later on, he walked away from the Lord. He was a comedian, and Jesus became the brunt of his jokes. He was really rude towards Jesus, but one day, he got into a terrible car accident and as he was dying, the people around him heard him speaking to Jesus. So even though he had bad things going on in his soul, his spirit was still purely connected to the Father by the blood of Jesus and he was on his way to heaven. He made it in. He may not have much for rewards—for doing good for Jesus—but he made it into heaven.

God is a spirit, and we were created in His image and likeness (Gen 1:26-27), so that also makes us spirits. Actually, in the Hebrew, it says we are speaking spirits. It is through our spirits that we connect with God. Our spirits and souls were created by God in heaven and placed into our bodies when we were conceived. It is in our souls where we feel happy, sad, mad, etc. It is in our souls where we are hurt by unkind words or feel blessed by kind loving words. It is where our personality exists that was given to us by our Father in heaven.

Our souls are the connector of our bodies with our spirits. It is like a valve between the two. Do you have the valve open, so there is a flow from the spirit through the soul to the body? Is your body being affected by the spirit, or is that valve shut? Are you ruling from your body or from your spirit? We cannot access the Holy Spirit through our emotions or our physical body, it is accessed through the Word of God by our spirit. When we believe the Word of God, our souls become renewed, transformed, and the valve opens more and more. The bad junk, lies, incorrect teachings, and bad memories are driven out and replaced with truth. As we grow in and respond to this truth, our minds, wills, and our physical bodies are affected. Depression will leave, healings will come, and addictions will be overcome because the spirit which is alive and filled with truth is more and more in control. It was the Holy Spirit that raised Jesus from the dead; that life-giving power now lives in your spirit if you've taken Jesus as Lord.

I have experienced this greatly in my life. At one time I was severely depressed and had a bad case of fibromyalgia. Why? Because I believed a lot of the devil's lies, which affected my soul, thereby affecting my physical body. As I grew in the knowledge and understanding of God's Word, learning who I was in Christ, learning I was loved by Jesus and His Father, and realizing I had the Holy Spirit living on the inside of me, I became physically and mentally healthier. I am still learning more and more to let my spirit, which is completely filled with the Holy Spirit, to rule in my life. I keep looking into the Bible, my spiritual mirror, to know who I really am.

As a natural mirror reflects our natural image, the Bible reflects our spiritual image. If you can trust a natural mirror to show you the real you, how much more should you trust the Bible to show you the real spiritual you? (James 1:23-25):

"For if you listen to the word and don't obey, it is like glancing at your face in a mirror. You see yourself, walk away, and forget what you look like. But if you look carefully into the perfect law that sets you free, and if you do what it says and don't forget what you heard, then God will bless you for doing it."

For God's Word is a spiritual mirror. It perfectly reflects who you are in the spirit. As you can't look directly into your face to see the real you, you can't look directly into your spirit either; you need a mirror to do that. You must look into the mirror and trust it. We have physical mirrors to see what we look like in the natural and we have a spiritual mirror, the Word of God, to show us what we look like in the spirit. Are you a reflection of what the Bible says you are? Are you a reflection of Jesus? You can be by studying, meditating on the Word, listening to anointed teachers, praying in the spirit, and being edified by the Spirit.

Again, connecting this to flagging, we want to be ruled by our spirits, following the flow of what the Holy Spirit wants us to do. We truly worship the Father through the

Holy Spirit. We do not worship through our emotions, for God is a spirit and we worship Him in spirit and truth. For our emotions can lead us in many directions, good or bad. You could be meditating on the love of God that would bring life and peace to your life or you could be meditating on what the devil is doing in your life, bringing in anger, frustration, condemnation, depression, and everything else destructive. Go to bed thinking about the good things of God in your life, and wake up thanking God for His existence in your life. Don't meditate on the devil and the thoughts he puts into your mind.

Dr. Caroline Leaf, a renowned neuroscientist, has studied the brain and the word of God and teaches on how the mind affects the body. She says we are made for love, the Father's love. When we think His thoughts we grow healthy "trees" in our brains. Our nerves actually look like trees. When we meditate on fear, worry, unforgiveness, or bitterness or speak nasty words out of our mouths, we grow wicked, crooked, malformed trees. The proteins used to grow new "trees" in our brains are not formed correctly when we don't think Godly thoughts. They don't live as long, they're not healthy, they're deformed. As we age, these wicked twisted trees decay faster and we can end up with holes in our memories. Memories just disappear, a cause for dementia in old age. However our brains are neuroplastic, meaning that they can repair themselves; so even in old age, you can grow new healthy memory trees to fill in the gaps and give you a better memory. You can do this by learning new things, new concepts in the Lord, or even learning a new language. Keep your mind on Him![9]

Chapter 7

Communion

One of the ways we praise and worship the Lord is through the practice of Communion. We remember who He is and what He did for us by His death, burial, and resurrection. We prophesy to the principalities and powers and to the heavenly hosts that we are believers in the Lord Jesus Christ. Jesus lived a sinless and spotless life. We prophesy when we take Communion in remembrance of His saving acts, to those heavenly entities, that we believe He gave Himself as a sacrificial lamb. We believe He allowed Himself to be beaten brutally, "skinned" at the hands of those whom He had created in the image of Himself, who is Love. This was the plan of redemption of man.

We prophesy to those principalities and powers that He allowed Himself to be nailed to a tree until dead, buried in a grave that wasn't His. We prophesy that His dead body received new life and rose up out of that grave on the third day, coming out of that grave with glory, honor, and power. When we do this, identifying ourselves with these acts, we are pulling into our lives the very resurrection power of the Lord Jesus Christ to heal, save, and prosper us in all aspects of life.

Communion is not only a physical act of eating a wafer or a piece of bread and drinking a little wine or grape juice. It is a powerful spiritual transaction when done in faith.

Chapter 7: Communion

For it has benefits for our lives and the lives of our families. Healing is in Communion, a blessing is in Communion, for the Zoe/God's life is in the blood. [10]

Let us look briefly at what the word *communion* means. Communion is a noun defined as:

- the sharing or exchanging of intimate thoughts and feelings, especially when the exchange is on a mental or spiritual level.
- the service of Christian worship at which bread and wine are consecrated and shared.[11]

In a sense, we are exchanging love with the Lord when we flag. We are honoring Him, loving Him; it is a spiritual exchange. Communion is fellowship.

Now let us look more at what people think of as Communion. It is when Jesus shared the Last Supper with His apostles in the upper room. Do you go into the upper room when you take communion, receiving it from Him? Imagine, when you take Communion, that Jesus is serving you just like He served them (Even when flagging, take yourself into that holy precious place of the upper room, where Jesus ministered to His disciples and loved on them, and allow Him to love on you).

First let's take a look at the Last Supper, the last Passover meal that Jesus spent with His apostles. Luke 22:7-20:

> *"Now the Festival of Unleavened Bread arrived, when the Passover lambs were sacrificed [Jesus, the true Passover Lamb, was sacrificed. He died at 3 pm, the same time as the Passover Lambs were being sacrificed. He was dying on the cross, outside the city gates of Jerusalem, as they were being sacrificed in the courtyard of the Temple]. Jesus sent Peter and John ahead and said, 'Go and prepare the Passover meal, so we can eat together.' 'Where do you want us to go?' they asked Him. He replied, 'As soon as you enter Jerusalem, a*

man carrying a pitcher of water will meet you. Follow him. At the house he enters, say to the owner, 'The Teacher asks, Where is the guest room where I can eat the Passover meal with my disciples?' He will take you upstairs to a large room that is already set up. That is the place. Go ahead and prepare our supper there.'" [The Lord has already prepared an upper room where we are to eat with Him at the Marriage Supper of the Lamb. It is a large guest room! Wherever He sends you to go minister for Him, that place has already been prepared. Keep your hearts open to follow the Spirit where He wants you to go, the place He has prepared, where He has provided favor, where He has prepared the people. He will send you if even only to minister to one person, for they are special to Him].

"Then at the proper time Jesus and His twelve apostles sat down together at the table." [Significant; at the proper time, stay in His timing! For in His timing, the work will be easy, for we are sitting down with Him]. "Jesus said, 'I have looked forward to this hour with deep longing, anxious to eat this Passover meal with you before my suffering begins.'" [How Jesus deeply longs to sit down with us, to have fellowship with us]. "'For I tell you now that I won't eat again until it comes to fulfillment in the Kingdom of God.' Then He took the cup of wine, and when He had given thanks for it, He said, 'Take this and share it among yourselves. For I will not drink wine again until the Kingdom of God has come.' Then He took a loaf of bread; and when He had thanked God for it, He broke it into pieces and gave it to His disciples saying, 'This is my body, given for you. Do this in remembrance of me.' After supper He took another cup of wine and said, 'This wine is a token of God's new covenant to save you - an agreement sealed with the blood I will pour out for you.'"

Chapter 7: Communion

Now we will look at the story in Matthew's gospel, Matt 26:17-30:

"On the first day of the Festival of Unleavened Bread, the disciples came to Jesus and asked, 'Where do you want us to prepare the Passover meal for you?'" [Don't be afraid to ask Him, inquire of the Holy Spirit, where to go]. *"'As you go into the city,' He told them, 'you will see a certain man. Tell him, 'The Teacher says: My time has come, and I will eat the Passover meal with My disciples at your house.' So the disciples did as Jesus told them and prepared the Passover meal there. When it was evening, Jesus sat down at the table with the Twelve. While they were eating, He said, 'I tell you the truth, one of you will betray me.'"* [We have all betrayed Him, but oh, how He loves us]. *"Greatly distressed, each one asked in turn, 'Am I the one, Lord?' He replied, 'One of you who has just eaten from this bowl with me will betray me. For the Son of Man must die, as the Scriptures declared long ago. But how terrible it will be for the one who betrays him. It would be far better for that man if he had never been born!' Judas, the one who would betray him, also asked, 'Rabbi, am I the one?' And Jesus told him, 'You have said it.' As they were eating, Jesus took some bread and blessed it. Then he broke it in pieces and gave it to the disciples, saying, 'Take this and eat it, for this is my body.' And he took a cup of wine and gave thanks to God for it. He gave it to them and said, 'Each of you drink from it, for this is my blood, which confirms the covenant between God and his people. It is poured out as a sacrifice to forgive the sins of many. Mark my words—I will not drink wine again until the day I drink it new with you in my Father's Kingdom.' Then they sang a hymn and went out to the Mount of Olives."*

Jesus has eaten His last supper with them. He now goes into the Garden of Gethsemane to pray before they come to take Him to crucify Him.

We see two parts to the meal, He took some bread, breaking it, representing His body broken, beaten, crucified for our diseases, our infirmities, and our sicknesses (Matt. 8:17). The bread is for the body; the bloodshed is for our redemption. We were healed when we were redeemed. Salvation is two parts. When we pray in the *Our Father* prayer, "give us this day our daily bread," it is referring to giving us our daily healing. Jesus is the bread of life. He was broken, battered, so we wouldn't have to be. Joseph Prince speaks about communion being a "proverbial fountain of youth." Just as bread is pounded, battered in the dough stage, then it is put into the fire, and the grapes are crushed and put into a dark place, Jesus was pounded, put into the fire, crushed, and put into a dark place before He became our bread and wine.

Let's now look at the story of the Syrophoenician woman regarding the healing of her daughter in Mark 7:24-29 NLT (why we can say the bread is our daily healing):

"Then Jesus left Galilee and went north to the region of Tyre. He didn't want anyone to know which house He was staying in, but He couldn't keep it a secret. Right away a woman who had heard about Him came and fell at His feet. Her little girl was possessed by an evil spirit, and she begged Him to cast out the demon from her daughter. Since she was a Gentile, born in Syrian Phoenicia, Jesus told her, 'First I should feed the children—My own family, the Jews. It isn't right to take food from the children and throw it to the dogs.' [Gentiles] She replied, 'That's true, Lord, but even the dogs under the table are allowed to eat the scraps from the children's plates.' 'Good answer!' He said. 'Now go home, for the demon has left your daughter.' And when she

arrived home, she found her little girl lying quietly in bed, and the demon was gone."

In the King James Version, verse 27 reads:

*"But Jesus said unto her, 'Let the children first be filled: for it is not meet to take the **children's bread**, and to cast it unto the dogs.'"*

This woman had come to Jesus to get her daughter healed and set free from a demonic spirit. And He says that He needs to feed the Jews—His own family—first. She wants healing, and He is talking about "food." A little confusing maybe, but she understood. She came for the healing of her daughter and she got what she wanted. She received "the children's bread," the healing of her daughter. The children's bread was the healing.

Disease is caused by the oppression of the devil. In Acts 10:38, we see this:

"And you know that God anointed Jesus of Nazareth with the Holy Spirit and with power. Then Jesus went around doing good and healing all who were oppressed by the devil, for God was with Him."

So when He cast out the devil, her child was healed. Also take note from this, that **it only takes a crumb to get you healed,** for the woman said even the dogs get to eat the crumbs. As when you light a candle from another candle, you don't dim the first candle; you only need a crumb to get healed. Jesus is both the light of the world and He is the living bread, broken for us. If you have faith the size of a mustard seed (which is small) in Him, you will be healed. She had faith and her child was healed.

Now let's look at the New Testament church, how Paul taught them to do communion. We will go to 1 Cor 11:23-29:

"For I pass on to you what I received from the Lord himself. On the night when He was betrayed, the

Lord Jesus took some bread and gave thanks to God for it. Then He broke it in pieces and said, 'This is My body, which is given for you. Do this in remembrance of Me.' In the same way, He took the cup of wine after supper, saying, 'This cup is the new covenant between God and his people—an agreement confirmed with My blood. Do this in remembrance of Me as often as you drink it.' Every time you eat this bread and drink this cup, you are announcing the Lord's death until He comes again. So anyone who eats this bread or drinks this cup of the Lord unworthily is guilty of sinning against the body and blood of the Lord. That is why you should examine yourself before eating the bread and drinking the cup. For if you eat the bread or drink the cup without honoring the body of Christ, you are eating and drinking God's judgment upon yourself. That is why many of you are weak and sick and some have even died."

Paul talks to them about examining themselves. He is referring to how they discern their taking of the body and blood of Jesus, not their sins. Because He "rode their case" about how some were eating and drinking the bread and wine, getting drunk and others were going hungry. 1 Cor 11:17-22:

"But in the following instructions, I cannot praise you. For it sounds as if more harm than good is done when you meet together. First, I hear that there are divisions among you when you meet as a church, and to some extent, I believe it. But, of course, there must be divisions among you so that you who have God's approval will be recognized! When you meet together, you are not really interested in the Lord's Supper. For some of you hurry to eat your own meal without sharing with others. As a result, some go hungry while others get drunk. What? Don't you

have your own homes for eating and drinking? Or do you really want to disgrace God's church and shame the poor? What am I supposed to say? Do you want me to praise you? Well, I certainly will not praise you for this!"

Paul is jumping on their case for their behavior, saying, really, why are you doing communion, anyway? You are fighting among yourselves, some are eating it all, some are going hungry, and others are getting drunk! Is this what Jesus did? Is this how He did the last supper He had with His disciples, doing communion and telling them to do the same in remembrance of Him? No! Paul then gives them proper instructions on how to do communion. It is not a ritual act! It is a REMEMBERING of His suffering and death for our healing and salvation.

When you do communion, get the elements ready. We use grape juice and a cracker, some use wine; if you only have water and a cookie, you can use it. You just need two elements to represent His body broken for us and His blood shed for our sins. Then picture Him bringing you the elements as He did the disciples, remembering His beatings and crucifixion. He suffered tremendously for us. Picture His dying on the cross. You don't need a priest or a pastor to have communion, as believers we are priests (1 Peter 2:9). You just need you and the two elements. Get yourself and elements ready and meditate on what Jesus did. Using your faith, take the bread and wine/juice/water in remembrance of His actions for you. As you take the bread, putting it in your mouth, it becomes Jesus healing you. You become bone of His bone, flesh of His flesh, allow His body to bring healing to your body. Thank Him for all He has done!

You can follow the words of Paul, but you can also follow the Spirit in doing communion. It is so important not to make it a ritualistic event, but to commune, have fellowship with Jesus as you remember what He did for you! You can do communion every day, or numerous times a day. If you are sick do communion as if you were taking a medication to get well. Communion has the power to get you well. Do it three times a day if need be, believing in the power of His sacrifice!

Here is an example of a prayer you can pray as you take Communion:

Take the bread in your hand and say:

"I do this in remembrance of what you did for me at the beating post, how you were tortured, beaten, bunched, slapped! I remember what was done to you, how your body was literally ripped apart for me. For by Your stripes I was completely healed (Isaiah 53:5, 1 Peter 2:24). I remember how your blood poured out on the ground as you were beaten. I prophesy to the principalities, powers, and rulers in high places that I believe in Your death, burial, and resurrection, and that You did this all for me. I believe and receive my healing.

Eat the bread.

Now take the cup in your hand and say:

I take this cup in remembrance of Your bloodshed on my behalf. I remember the horrendous death you suffered on the cross for me. I thank you, Jesus, for this New Covenant that was cut in Your blood. For Your blood has brought me complete forgiveness and washed me free from every sin. I thank you, Jesus, that Your shed blood has made me righteous, in right standing now with our Father. As I drink this wine, I celebrate all that You have done for me, and I now partake of My inheritance which is preservation, healing, wholeness, and prosperity.

Drink the wine or grape juice.

Thank you, Jesus, for all you have done for me, for I love you because You loved me first.

Part 2: The Mechanics of Flag Making

Chapter 8

Types of Flags, Rods, Moves

As I spoke about in part one, flagging is worship! We flag to an audience of one: the Lord. We worship His Presence, because His Presence is Jesus, and His Presence is everything. For it is in His Presence that all that of our needs are supplied, His power, His healing, His mercy, His faithfulness, and His provision. In the presence of Jesus, we not only have Jesus but His Father and His Spirit, the Holy Spirit. Praying and praising Him with our flags brings His Presence, therefore bringing in His power, and His glory, to get done what He wants to be done. Expect that power and His glory to manifest as we worship and He does the rest.

Think about this scripture from The Passion Translation Heb 13:15:

> *"So we no longer offer up a steady stream of blood sacrifices, but through Jesus, we will offer up to God a steady stream of praise sacrifices—these are 'the lambs' we offer from our lips that celebrate his name!"*

Our praises are "the lambs," the sacrifices that are offered up to God. Praise drives out darkness and brings down walls, just like in the story of Jericho. The Israelites shouts brought down those thick walls of Jericho, and they didn't even touch them; their praise brought them down. Praise

Chapter 8: Types of Flags, Rods, Moves

down the walls in your life.

As we praise and worship with our flags, it is more about what is in our hearts than what the colors of the flags are or the type of music you are listening to. It is about connecting with laser-like focus, seeking the Presence, Jesus, following the leading of the Holy Spirit, who lives now on the inside of you if you are born again.

There are many steps to making flags. You will want to determine what type of flag(s) you want, the rod size/diameter and length, the colors of the flags, the name of your flags, and scriptural references related to the meaning of your flags. I will describe the different types of rods used in making flags and a basic movement related to the use of the flag. Included will be some basic instructions I have used on how to make your own flags, where to get supplies (including references), and places where to find information.

Getting started: There a number of different types of worship flags. There are flex flags/quill flags, swing flags, banners/veils, spin flags, and angel wings. There are also worship spinners and tabrets, but my instructions will focus on flags. Flex flags are flags that fit on a rod, with both ends of the flag pocket closed. Swing flags don't have a rod; they are weighted with a "handle" and work better in smaller spaces. Banners or veils/billows are longer flags that billow as you move them. You can add a pole to a banner and use it that way or you can take the end of the banner and whip it up and down, giving it movement. Spin flags spin on the rod. Both ends of the pocket are left open, and the rod slides through the pocket spinning around in the pocket. This flag is also good for tight spaces because you can hold it up over your head, eliminating contact with anything lower, especially like one lady said, "she could flag above the heads of children down in front of her." Angel wing flags have a more rounded appearance than the square or rectangle flags. Swallowtail flags have a "V" shape at the bottom end of the flag or you can make your flag with a number of tails looking like flames. Be as creative as you want or are inspired to be.

I mostly have flex flags, as I really couldn't connect with the swing flags, but I have made myself some spin flags as well. My husband truly enjoys flagging, and he has angel wings plus rectangle flags, and some are much larger flags than I use. I am a silk flag person, but my husband has flags made from a number of different materials. Since he is stronger, using the heavier material isn't as much of an issue for him. The weight of the rods makes a difference as well; the lighter the material in the flag, the lighter the rod you can use. Wooden dowel rods and some of the thicker fiberglass or acrylic rods can get to be quite heavy.

Flex flags have movement with the rod; they flex! The smaller the rod the more flexible they are. Quill rods are small-sized diameter rods, with a lot of flex, you can actually bend them in half for storage or travel. You can fold a quill rod flag, wrap your flag around it, tucking the end inside the "pocket." One thing to remember is never, ever leave flex rod flags in a hot vehicle, for they can warp or break. Leave all flex rods lying flat in the vehicle.

Flex rods (0.098 - 0.112 in diameter) have about 20% flex, quill/quiver rods (0.080) have about 50% flex, so you can see they are much more bendy. If you put a quill or super flexible rod in a larger heavier flag, they can really bend and make them more difficult to maneuver. I like to use quill rods in 5mm or 8mm 36" x 45" silk flags. You can get the fiberglass rods from Goodwinds.com, and you can get acrylic rods from TapPlastics.com—plastic rods, tubes, and shapes. They have many sizes; just make sure you get vinyl end caps as well. When cutting a fiberglass rod, wrap a piece of tape around the rod first, then cut; this helps to eliminate fiberglass splinters in your fingers, for they are difficult to remove. Using end caps will help keep the rods from poking through the ends of the rod pockets of your flags. I have put links in the reference section for these products.

Some people prefer wooden dowels for rods as well. They come in different lengths and sizes. They are good for fast flagging, for they drag very little and the wood cuts through the air instead of dragging, but they are less graceful at a slower pace and can be somewhat heavier (information from Andrea York's video, "Worship Flags: What Kind of Poles" link in the reference section).

Next, I will cover some basic concepts on using your flags; these ideas I learned from Andrea York in her video on "Three Tips for Beginners" (there is a link in the reference section).

Start off with only a single flag.

Use your dominant arm.

As you progress, you can add a second flag using your other arm. But it is much easier to get the "hang" of flagging by using just one arm first. I actually use only one arm—my dominant one—quite a bit. That way, when my major arm gets tired, I just switch over to my other arm and give the dominant one a break. Another reason for only using a single flag is some of my flags are heavier, especially my triple white, which is three layers of different types of silk and is one of my larger flags. Or, I may have only one flag of that size and color, but I have mixed and matched flags together of different sizes and colors when flagging. After I got more used to flagging, I have even held two different flex flags in one hand, putting them in between my fingers. I like to use my solid "gold" flags together with my yellow, orange, and red "Firebrand" flags to give more impact!

Flag using the figure "8", the infinity symbol. All the action is in the wrist. To understand how to do some basic moves watch Andrea York's video called "How to Use

Worship Flags: Five Moves to Get You Started"; the link is found in the reference section.

Personally, I just "move" with the flag, waving it in correspondence to what I am feeling in my spirit. I don't do choreographed worship dance. As I have mentioned before, my husband has really one basic move, a slow wave back and forth, so don't feel intimidated that you need to learn a bunch of moves and do them correctly to worship the Lord. Remember it is what is in your heart that is important, not what you do with the flag.

Another important aspect of flagging is to pay attention to where you are! What are you going to hit! Are you making people "cold" with the breeze from the waving of your flag! Is the space big enough? If you are flagging in a smaller space, try using a smaller flex flag or use a spin flag that you can hold up and spin, thereby protecting all who are around you. Or using a swing flag that doesn't have a rod. I have gone up in a balcony in a church to be out of the way. Make sure you pay attention to your surroundings as you flag as not to hit anyone or anything with your flag. If you are going to flag in a church, get permission to do so first. Honor the authority in that church or ministry.

Also a quick comment on lending out your flags; you don't have to feel guilty about not lending them out. They are special to you and they do cost money. Not everyone will take care of them as you do, so even though people may come up and ask to use them, you have the right to say no. Another thing is: don't leave them behind in a church, thinking they will be safe; people have "lost" them that way. If they belong to you, take them home. If they belong to the church, also keep them in a safe place, for not everyone who comes to church is honest. Sad but true.

Chapter 9

Colors, Naming, Scriptural References

All color has its own voice, so what are you saying with your flag? What do you want to proclaim?

I will attempt to give a composite of some of the color meanings I have found. I give references to my sources in my reference section. There are lots of resources out there on flagging, including the internet.

Basic colors:

Red: The blood of Jesus (Eph 1:7); Redemption (Is 63:2-4); Salvation; Sacrifice of Christ's blood (Rom 3:25); Atonement (Lev 14:52-53); Fervent love; Life (Lev 17:11); Consuming fire; Courage; Power; Warfare (Nahum 2:3); Power (Rev 6:4)

Purple: Royalty (Esther 8:15); Kingship (John 19:12); Beauty (Esther 27:37); Priesthood; Majesty; Wealth; Reigning with Christ; Creativity; Mediator.

White: Holy, Victorious, Worthy (Rev 1:4); Bride of Christ (Rev 3:4-50); Cleanse (Ps 51:7); Glory, Light and Holy Spirit (Matt 3:16); Ancient of Days (Daniel 7:9); Purity & Holiness (Dan 12:10); Honor and Righteousness (Rev 19:7)

Green: Healing (Rev 22:1-2); Life (John 15:5); Fruitful (Ps 92:12-13); Prosperity (Ps 92:14); Growth (Gen 9:3); Hope;

Peace; Victory; Health/Vitality (Gen 1:30); Restoration (Ps 23:2-3); New Beginnings (Is 27:6, Rom 6:4); Praise; Freshness.

Yellow: Glory of God (Rom 4:20); Friendship; Sunshine; Sonshine; Joy (Ps 21:6); Light (John 8:12); Holiness; Eternal Deity; Anointing (Ex 25:16); Happiness.

Blue: Kingship; Royalty (Esther 8:15); Priesthood; Revelation; Authority; Heaven; Holy Spirit; Divinity; Serenity; Tranquility; Patience; Communication; Healing; Blessings, Holy, Reminds us of where God is and how large He is.

Orange: Consuming Fire (Deut 4:24); Lion of Judah (Rev 5:5); Praise (Eph 3:19); Judgement (2 Thess. 1:6-7); Holy Spirit (Acts 2:3-4); Deliverance (Dan 3:19-29); Joy; Warrior (Ps 97:3); Spiritual warfare/Intercession; Harvest; Endurance; Fire.

Brown: Humility (Esther 4:3); People (Is 40:7-8); Earth; Worshipping; Confession (Neh. 91:1-3); Devotion; Humanity; Earthen vessels.

Black: Mystery of God (Dan 2:19); Darkness (Eph 5:11); Mourning (Jer 8:21); Famine, Affliction, Calamity (Lam 4:8, Rev 6:5, Jer 8:21); Righteous Judgement; Darkness (Jos. 24:7); Sin; Evil.

Gray: Glory and Power of God (Rev 15:8); Smoke (Rev 8:4); Old Age; Dignity; Honor; Repentance.

Pink (Rose): Glory; Rose of Sharon; New Life; Kingliness; Father's Heavenly Care; Feminine; Intimacy; Child-like Faith; Tenderness: God's Embrace.

Bronze/Brass: Forgiveness (Numbers 21:9); Sacrifice (John 3:14-15); Judgement of Sins; Testing by Fire (Num 21:17); Altar.

Silver: Strength; Redemption (Number 18:15-16; Luke 15:8); Refined; Words of the Lord (Ps 12:6); Words of

Righteousness; Wisdom; Purifier (Ps 66:10, Mal 3:3); God's Refining Process (Ps 66:10)

Gold: God's Glory (Ex 37); Divinity; Praise; Glory & Honor (1 Peter 1:7; Ex 37:40; Rev 1:13-14); Kingship (Esther 8:4); Refiner (Mal 3:3); Majesty (Esther 8:15); Power; Presence; Wisdom (Prov 25:12)

Combinations of Colors by Color: Colors can be used in combination to symbolize various Biblical truths.

Rainbow Colors: Covenant (Gen 9:13); Promise.

Red/Gold/Silver: Refine (Zech 13:9)

Blue/Aqua/Turquoise/White: Healing water (Ps 1:1-3; Rev 22:1)

Orange/Yellow/Red: Fire; Holy Spirit (Acts 2); Praise; Glory; Honor (1 Peter 1:18, Ps 79:5, Song of Songs 8:6); Guidance & protection (Ex 13:21, Ps 78:14)

Blue/Purple/Scarlet/Gold: Priesthood (1 Peter 2:9, Exodus 39:1); Kingship of God (Ex 25); Tabernacle (Ex 28:5)

Black/White: Clear cut; sharply defined; write it down.

Red/White/Blue: Liberty; Freedom.

Red/Purple/Blue: Used in the Tabernacle.

Red/Yellow/Blue: Primary colors, represent the Trinity.

Silver & Gold: Wealth; Luxury; Beauty.

Red/White: God's purifying work; The blood (red) and holiness (white)

Red/Gold/Green: Faith (gold); Hope (green); Love (red)

Reflective Material: Wherever the King Jesus shines, He brings light.

All Colors: Jubilee (Lev 25:9-10)

Combinations of Colors by Truth:

The Royalty of Christ/The Priesthood of the Believer: (Rev 1:6); Plum, Grape, Purple, Orchid, White.

Holy Fire/Baptism in the Holy Spirit: (Acts 2:3-4); Wine, Orange, Red, Yellow, White.

Covenant: (Gen 9:13); Red, Yellow, Blue, Orange, Green, Purple.

Tabernacle: (Ex 25:1-8, 28:5-12); Gold, Bronze, Purple, White, Scarlet, Blue & Silver.

Bride: White, Silver, Iridescence.

Royalty: Purple, Red.

River of God: Blue, Aqua, Silver.

Majesty: Purple, Red, Gold.

The Fire of God: Gold, Red, Yellow.

Israel: Silver, Blue.

Rainbow/Glory of God/Covenant Promises: Ezek 1:28, Gen 9:13, Red, Yellow, Orange, Purple, Indigo, Blue, Green.

Intercession: White, Silver, Gold.

I give a name and a scriptural reference to all the flags I make; even the ones I have purchased have a name and reference. Naming your flag(s) adds more meaning and character to the flag. My Firebrand flags are yellow, orange, and red, representing the Holy Spirit. I have made a two-piece purple and pink scissortail flag I called "Pure Joy." My reference scripture is Eph 3:14; *"He is our pure joy!"* My rainbow-colored flag I made I called "Covenant," my reference scripture being Gen 9:9; *"I hereby confirm my covenant with you and your descendants."* God told Noah He would never again destroy the earth, and He made a covenant with man and blessed him. I made a scissortail white and red flag that I called "Blood Washed Bride," red for the blood and white for the bride, the church. My scripture reference is Gal 3:13 NLT; *"But Christ rescued us from the curse pronounced by the law. When He hung on the cross, He took upon Himself the curse for our wrongdoing."*

Chapter 9: Colors, Naming, Scriptural References

Giving your flag a title and reference helps you to focus during your worship.

I also use my triple white flag to praise Him for His holiness, His righteousness. When I focus on the Holy Spirit, I like to use my "Firebrand" and my "Glory" (solid yellow/gold) flags together. My liberty flags are my red, white and blue ones, thanking Him for our freedom and liberty and claiming our future freedom and liberty. I have used this pair in our hometown parade and when my husband and I did a Veteran's day program at a local nursing home.

Chapter 10

How to Make a Basic Flag

In this chapter, I will give some step-by-step instructions on how to make your very own flag. Materials you will need are:

1) Fabric. I like silk, either 5 or 8 mm silk from Dharma Trading Co. (https://www.dharmatrading.com/). They have wonderful silk; it floats so nicely. They also carry other fabrics that you can buy in different widths and yardages. My preferred flag size is 36" wide and 45" long. To make a set of flags this size, you will need to buy 2 yards of 45" silk and cut it in half, one yard (36") for each flag. Another feature I like is that you can buy a veil and cut it in half and you will have two flags that are already hemmed. Then you only have to deal with the raw edge where you will add your "ribbon" for your rod pocket. I have also purchased their 21.5" x 21.5" scarves for smaller square flags. Some flag makers use a number of different types of materials: chiffons, satins, lames, polyesters; you will want something that will flow/float nicely. I have been given square nylon scarves that I used to make flags for children. Another option is to look for pretty scarves in a thrift store or at thrift sales to make flags out of; however, it is best if the color(s) are the same on both sides of the scarf.

2) For my rod pockets, I buy different colors and widths of the grosgrain ribbon. It is a sturdier cross-grain ribbon,

Chapter 10: How to Make a Basic Flag

thus helping to prevent your rods from poking through the ends. With my quill rods and flex rods, I buy 1.5" ribbon. I have also purchased a 3" ribbon for a larger pocket for a spin rod.

3) I sew with either silk thread or 100% cotton thread.

By hemming your flags before dying, your thread will also be dyed, thereby eliminating the need for multiple spools of different colored threads. I use a small tight zigzag stitch to hem; a serger would probably give a nicer edge, but I don't have one. I just trim off my edges to make them look nicer after stitching. Don't like hemming? Get a veil, cut it in half; it is a little more expensive, but eliminates having to hem, which is a plus. To buy a veil go to DharmaTrading.com, then search for Habotai silk veils. To get a 35" x 42" set of flags, buy the 35" x 84" veil. If you have never sewed on silk before, began with the 8mm; it is a little heavier. I have included a reference to a video on how to sew with silk since it is a thinner, silkier fabric, making sewing with it is a little trickier.

4) To dye the silk, you will need some citric acid to pretreat the silk, this helps the dye to set. You can buy it from Dharma Trading Co. or Amazon. I use four teaspoons in a quart of water. You soak your silk for about 5-10 minutes, then squeeze out, but do not rinse out.

5) I use Dharma Trading's Fiber Reactive Procion Dyes. If you use acid dyes, you have to heat the fabric and cook it in a microwave to set the dye. It will give a brighter color but it is more work, and I don't have a separate microwave to use. Dharma Trading has lots of colors to choose from. Depending on the size of your flags, you will get quite a few flags dyed from one container of dye. I also like to dye cotton t-shirts, dresses, and pants that I sew for my granddaughters with this dye as well. But with cotton, you need to use washing soda/soda ash for setting the dye. You can use it on silk, too, but it is harsher to the silk than citric acid. Some people use vinegar for setting; it is another weak

acid. I have posted how-to videos and pictured instructions in the reference section.

6) To ice dye, you will need some pans and ice. You will need to cover the piece of material totally with ice before putting on the dye (I have seen a post about adding the dye first, then ice, but haven't tried it yet). I've bought some plastic rectangular baskets at Dollar Tree to set my material in, then I set that in a pan so that my material doesn't lay in the melted dye water/water from the melting ice.

To have matching flags, you will want to dye both pieces of material together. To do that, just fold your material (two yards of 45" x 36" for two 36" wide flags) in half before dying and cut later, or cut and leave both pieces together. If you don't want the flags to match, then dye them separately.

Okay, let's get started:

You will want to decide what color(s), (corresponding to what your focus for the flag is) of dyes you want to use, and where you want to apply the dyes on the material. Have a sort of concept of what you want your flag to look like when finished. With ice dying, you don't really know what they will look like when finished, but that is also the exciting part, to see what you get when your ice is melted, and you undo them.

Then decide how you want to fold, scrunch, or twist the material. Twisting, scrunching, folding will give you different patterns (I bought some silk scarves and practiced first, trying different methods of scrunching to see how they would turn out, to figure out what I liked best).

Soak your silk for 5-10 minutes in a citric acid bath, take and squeeze out excess liquid but DO NOT RINSE!

Place the bunched up, twisted, scrunched up silk in your drainer basket. You will want your drainer basket resting in another pan but not sitting on the bottom, for you want room for drainage.

Chapter 10: How to Make a Basic Flag

Fully cover it with pieces of ice (I have re-added ice later if I see chunks of dye left on the material; this helps to dissolve the extra dye, making for easier rinsing later).

Sprinkle on the dye(s).

Let sit until the ice melts. I have done it outside, setting the pan on the warm sidewalk or in our basement when the weather outside is too cold.

After the ice has all melted, remove the silk from the basket, unfold and rinse with water until the water runs clear. Some dyes rinse out better with warm to hot water, especially the turquoise blue.

(Note: It won't harm the flags if they sit longer even after the ice melts).

I like to iron my silks while they are damp.

Now to sew on the rod pocket. There are a couple of ways of adding the rod pocket, either by gluing it partially on and then finish sewing it, or pinning and sewing it on in one step. To glue silk to grosgrain ribbon, lay the grosgrain ribbon on a flat surface, apply a "thin row" of fabric glue, then place the top of the unhemmed 36" edge of the silk on the bottom edge of the ribbon where you have applied the glue (You will need about 37" of ribbon, that gives you a half-inch for a hem on each end). Let dry.

To hem the edges, fold the grosgrain ribbon over towards the inside, stitching it down. Now fold the grosgrain ribbon over the top of glued on silk, pin and sew in place, creating a pocket for the rod. As I have gotten better at it, I just pin the silk and ribbon together, with the silk on the inside of the ribbon creating the rod pocket. Depending on what kind of flag you are making, just sew up one end of the pocket before adding the rod, then sew up the other end. If you are making a spin flag, you will need to leave both ends open for the rod to slide through.

You only need to hem three sides of your material, as the fourth side is connected to the grosgrain ribbon for the rod pocket.

I have added links in the reference section from Dharma Trading with pictures of how to ice dye (this is for cotton dying, but it is relatively the same concepts) and on how to make a spin rod.

Happy Flagging!

Chapter 11

References for Making or Purchasing Flags

Flag & Information Websites:

- Worship Warriors: https://worshipwarriors.net/
- It's About Worship: https://www.itsaboutworship.com/
- Catch the Fire: https://catchthefireworshipflags.com/
- Victory Hill Flags: https://www.etsy.com/shop/VictoryHillFlags
- All For His Glory: https://www.allforhisgloryministries.net/
- Worship Flag Store: https://www.worshipflagstore.com/index.php?p=home
- Spirit Fire Silks: https://www.etsy.com/shop/SpiritFireSilks?ref=condensed_trust_header_title_items
- Worship Expressions: https://www.worshipexpressions.net/
- Dyed4You: https://dyed4you.com/blog/
- Flags for Faith: https://www.flagsforfaith.com/
- Called to Flag: https://www.calledtoflag.com/
- Praise and Worship Flags - Making Flags by CreationsAnewFl https://hubpages.com/art/CreationsAnew_Flag_Making
- Waves of Worship, Purpose & Use: http://www.wavesofworshipflagministry.com/Purpose---Use.html

There are lots of flaggers and flagging community groups on Facebook. For more information check out Flagging: An Audience Unto One Facebook's page as well. Link on Facebook: https://www.facebook.com/loofmawr/

Rods:

Fiberglass rods - Goodwinds.com: https://goodwinds.com/carbon-fiberglass/fiberglass/solid-fiberglass.html

Vinyl cap ends for rods: https://goodwinds.com/catalog/connectors/vinyl-end-caps.html

Acrylic rods & capons: https://www.tapplastics.com/product/plastics/plastic_rods_tubes_shapes

How-To Sites/YouTube videos:

- Tamara Warta - How to make dance streamers: https://dance.lovetoknow.com/How_to_Make_Dance_Streamers
- Andrea York - 3 Tips for Beginners for Dancing with Worship Flags: https://www.youtube.com/watch?v=-OXWy4mT264
- Andrea York - Worship Flags - What kind of Poles (wood, flexion, or quiver) is best? https://www.youtube.com/watch?v=pP8j79mzY9k
- Andrea York - How to Use Worship Flags - 5 moves to get you started: https://www.youtube.com/watch?v=5gI-J5By1aI
- Andrea York - How to Use Silk Swing Flags & Prophetic Silk Banners/Veils: https://www.youtube.com/watch?v=aR8NHR3fr14
- Melanie Price - How to Make a Spinning Flagpole from Start to Finish: https://www.youtube.com/watch?v=TxGUfzMmSOs&feature=share
- Dyed for You - The Differences Between Quills,

Chapter 11: References for Making or Purchasing Flags

Bendies, and Spinners: https://www.youtube.com/watch?v=o1tzrXZNYgw
- Fire Catchers Classroom - Andrea York: https://catchthefireworshipflags.com/ignite/fire-catchers-classroom
- Ramona Helfer - How to make spinner rods for your flags: https://www.facebook.com/ramona.helfer/videos/10211118099288426/

Colors:

- http://dyed4you.com/blog/about-our-silks/colors/
- https://www.worshipexpressions.net/biblical-color-symbolism.html
- https://www.itsaboutworship.com/symbolism-of-colors/
- https://catchthefireworshipflags.com/colors

How to Dye & Sew Silk:

- How to tie-dye silk: https://www.youtube.com/watch?v=d4HAHG09CQU&list=LLwWYhPxMrx7Dy2HVekOlsjQ&index=3&t=0s
- How to: Sewing with Silk/Slippery Fabrics: https://www.youtube.com/watch?v=m9nC8ZPfLfc
- How to ice dye fabric: https://www.youtube.com/watch?v=MY746UKWz7c
- How to dye a silk scarf - The Easy Microwave Way (for acid dyeing): https://www.youtube.com/watch?v=YEsrZpGaV1Q
- How to Dye Fabric: Ice Dyeing: https://www.youtube.com/watch?v=L7EEWdL7etI
- Learn How To Ice Dye - Very good tutorial with pictures: https://www.dharmatrading.com/home/learn-how-to-ice-dye.html?lnav=default.html

Other References & Resources:

- "Praise and Worship with Flags, Waging Spiritual Warfare in the Church and Home", Delores Hillman Harris, Westbow Press, A Division of Thomas Nelson, 1663 Liberty Drive, Bloomington, IN 47403
- "The Authority of the Believer", John A. MacMillian, Wing Spread Publishers, 3825 Hartzdale Drive, Camp Hill, PA 17011
- "The Believer's Authority, What you didn't learn in church", Andrew Wommack, Harrison House Publishers, P.O. Box 35035, Tulsa, OK 74153
- "The Believer's Authority", Kenneth E. Hagin, Faith Library Publications, Kenneth Hagin Ministries, P.O. 50126, Tulsa, OK 50126
- "Spirit, Soul & /Body", Andrew Wommack, Harrison House Publishers, P.O. Box 35035, Tulsa, OK 74153
- "The New You & The Holy Spirit", Andrew Wommack, Harrison House Publishers, P.O. Box 35035, Tulsa, OK 74153
- "Destined To Reign", Joseph Prince, Harrison House Publishers, P.O. Box 35035, Tulsa, OK 74153, Joseph Prince Teaching Resources
- "Health and Wholeness Through The Holy Communion, Joseph Prince, Joseph Prince Resources, www.JosephPrince.com
- "The Blood and the Glory", Billye Brim, Harrison House Publishers, P.O. Box 35035, Tulsa, OK 74153
- "How You Can Pray In The End of Days and my call to help the pray-ers," Billye Brim, A Glorious Church Fellowship, Inc., Billye Brim Ministries, Prayer Mountain in the Ozarks, P.O. Box 40, Branson, MO 65615
- "The Names of God", Marilyn Hickey, Marilyn Hickey Ministries, P.O. Box 17340, Denver, CO 80217

- "The Holy Spirit And You" A Study Guide To The Spirit-filled Life, Dennis & Rita Bennett, Bridge-Logos Publishers, P.O. Box 141630, Gainsville, FL 32614
- "Spiritual Authority", CD series, Terry Mize Ministries, P.O. Box 35044, Tulsa, OK 74153, www.terrymizeministries.org

Endnotes

1   https://catchthefireworshipflags.com/fire-catchers-classroom, 2019-09-14 Fire Catchers Classroom:Elevate Your Praise

2   Revival Radio TV interview with Michael Miller, https://www.youtube.com/watch?v=L9dDIIXqF4E&t=1s

3   https://catchthefireworshipflags.com/fire-catchers-classroom, 2019-09-14 Fire Catchers Classroom: Elevate Your Praise

4   https://catchthefireworshipflags.com/ignite/fire-catchers-classroom "Going Deeper in God"

5   https://www.facebook.com/rosie.a.bowden/videos/10158956021888782/

6   Webster's New World College Dictionary, 4th Edition, Copyright 2007 Michael Agnes, Editor in Chief, Wiley Publishing, Inc., Cleveland, Ohio

7   Webster's New World College Dictionary, 4th Edition, Copyright 2007 Michael Agnes, Editor in Chief, Wiley Publishing, Inc., Cleveland, Ohio

8   Spiritual Authority, CD series, Terry Mize Ministries, P.O. Box 35044, Tulsa, OK 74153, www.terrymizeministries.org,

9   "Who Switched Off My Brain? Controlling toxic thoughts and emotions" Dr. Caroline Leaf, Copyright 2007, Switch On Your Brain International LLC, 2140 E Southlake Blvd., Suite L#809, Southlake, TX 76092

10   Communion: Secrets of the Last Days, White Dove Ministries https://www.youtube.com/watch?v=KzZHbi2mqiE

11   Dictionary.com

www.ingramcontent.com/pod-product-compliance
Lightning Source LLC
Chambersburg PA
CBHW060340080526
44584CB00013B/859